DATE			

Rachel Carson

Twayne's United States Authors Series

Frank Day, Editor
Clemson University

TUSAS 619

Rachel Carson near her summer home in Maine. ©1961 by Eric Hartmann. Used by permission of Rachel Carson Council, Inc.

Rachel Carson

Mary A. McCay

Loyola University

Twayne Publishers ■ New York

Maxwell Macmillan Canada ■ Toronto

Maxwell Macmillan International ■ New York Oxford Singapore Sydney

Rachel Carson
Mary A. McCay

Copyright 1993 by Twayne Publishers

Excerpts from unpublished correspondence and notes of Rachel Carson used by permission of Frances Collin, Trustee.

Twayne Publishers   Maxwell Macmillan Canada, Inc.
Macmillan Publishing Company   1200 Eglinton Avenue East
866 Third Avenue   Suite 200
New York, New York 10022   Don Mills, Ontario M3C 3N1

Macmillan Publishing Company is part of the Maxwell Communications Group of Companies.

Library of Congress Cataloging-in-Publication Data

McCay, Mary A.
    Rachel Carson / Mary A. McCay
    p.   cm. – (Twayne's United States authors series; TUSAS 619)
    Includes bibliographical references and index.
    ISBN 0-8057-3988-2
    1. Carson, Rachel, 1907-1964 – Literary art. 2. Ecologists – United States – Biography. 3. Environmentalists – United States – Biography. 4. Science writers – United States – Biography. I. Title. II. Series.
QH31.C33M34   1993
574'.092 – dc20
[B]   92-39795
                                                                                     CIP
                                                                                      AC

The paper used in this publication meets the minimum requirements of American National Standard for Information Sciences – Permanence of Paper for Printed Library Materials, ANSI Z39.48-1984.

10 9 8 7 6 5 4 3 2

Printed in the United States of America.

For Douglas

and for Ellen Powers and John Swan

Contents

Preface

Most studies of Rachel Carson take the view that the research and writing of *Silent Spring* (1962) is the most compelling feature of her life and work. On the surface, this, her last book, strikes a dissonant cord with her benign earlier books about the sea and seems out of character with pictures of the petite, reserved woman wading through tide pools or holding binoculars too large for her small hands. *Silent Spring* was not just a single act of courage, however, it was the natural outcome of all the work Carson had done both as a scientist and as a writer. Her ecological stand in her last book is the natural outcome of Carson's earliest wish to teach people about the sea so they would respect its creatures and would understand that the oceans could not be exploited endlessly without terrible cost. She was from childhood – when she criticized her brother's rabbit hunting – to her last days a woman who believed that people had to understand their relationship with nature, not simply to preserve the natural world but to save themselves.

At the core of Carson's writing are the themes of interconnectedness and material immortality, as evidenced in the following passage from "Undersea," an article published in the *Atlantic* (1937) that became the heart of her first book, *Under the Sea Wind:* "Individual elements are lost to view, only to reappear again and again in different incarnations in a kind of material immortality. Kindred forces to those which, in some period inconceivably remote, gave birth to that primeval bit of protoplasm tossing on the ancient seas, continue their mighty and incomprehensible work. Against this cosmic background the life span of a particular plant or animal appears, not as a drama complete in itself, but only as a brief interlude in the panorama of endless change." Carson illustrates in that early article a pattern that persists in her writing. As it had for Melville and Conrad, the sea became Carson's focus and finally her greatest symbol. Its creative power and destructive force, its magnitude and infinite variety drew her. The ocean became the medium through which Carson spoke to the world.

The success of Carson's next book, *The Sea around Us* (1951), enabled her to retire from government work and devote all her time to research on the tidal areas that became the focus of her next book, *The Edge of the Sea* (1955). Carson wanted the book to be more than a seashore guide, Bob Hines, its illustrator, recalls. A book about the seashore, she believed, needed to do more than simply list flora and fauna. She wanted to show the way in which all the shore species were a part of a force at once creative and destructive, powerful and vulnerable, but never random. A small crab became symbolic of the delicate balance of all species in nature: "The little crab alone with the sea became a symbol that stood for life itself – for the delicate, destructible, yet incredibly vital force that somehow holds its place amid the harsh realities of the inorganic world."

The precarious balance of life in the natural world was to impress Carson again and again as she struggled with *Silent Spring*. Clearly, some species were not surviving the onslaught of DDT and other toxins contained in the herbicides and pesticides used widely in the two decades following World War II. Carson, in a sense, found herself in the position of the crab. In failing health, she held on, conducting her research, writing to colleagues, gathering more evidence, so that when the book was finished, though the writer would be nearly spent, the work would be unassailable. Her goal in *Silent Spring* was to document the destructive side effects of DDT on the natural world in language laypeople could understand and thereby change the way they thought about that world.

Carson planned to set the danger to humans from indiscriminate pesticide and herbicide use within the larger structure of danger to the whole ecosystem. Human control of nature for human comfort or efficiency did not always work to the advantage of the people who believed they were in control; ironically, efforts to control crop damage by insects and weed growth were inflicting unintended damage on the surrounding environment and on human beings. By 1959 Carson was beginning to document not just casual or careless poisonings but a cumulative toxic buildup with the potential to alter the function of nearly every living cell. DDT was not just killing birds; it could eventually kill us all.

Shirley Briggs, Carson's co-worker and the director of the Rachel Carson Council, has pointed out that Carson's message applied "to far more than just pesticides." Indeed, it applied to the attitude that

Americans, as citizens of an industrialized nation, had adopted toward nature. This message links all the earlier books to *Silent Spring*. The crude and brutish treatment of the environment for profit had long been a concern for Carson: she observed it in coal mining enterprises in her native Pennsylvania, and she observed it in the fishermen off Georges Bank when she was researching her books about the sea. Finally, she observed it in the U.S. government's policies on pesticides and weed killers. What Carson's books do, besides speaking eloquently on behalf of nature, is to highlight the ways in which humans fail to appreciate it.

Acknowledgments

This book would not have been possible without the help of Douglas McCay and the following people: Julie Guidry, Ray McGowan, Melanie McKay, Betsy Pedersen, Kimberly St. germaine, Sophia Stone, Charlie Thomas, Susan Tucker, and Donna Glee Williams.

I would also like to thank the Loyola Grants and Leave Committee for allocating the money for me to travel to the Beinecke Library and to the Rachel Carson Council to do research. Shirley Briggs of the Rachel Carson Council was most helpful in letting me see letters and manuscripts in her possession and in talking to me about her work with Carson. She consented to be interviewed when I went to the Rachel Carson Council to work.

Permission to quote from the Rachel Carson Collection was granted by the Beinecke Library at Yale University and by the Frances Collin Literary Agency.

Chronology

1907	Rachel Louise Carson born 27 May in Springdale, Pennsylvania, the third child of Robert Warden Carson and Maria Frazier (McLean) Carson.
1913	Enters Springdale Grammar School. Teachers note frequent absences, but Carson still excels.
1918	Publishes prize-winning first story in *St. Nicholas* magazine; others follow.
1921	Enters Springdale High School.
1923	Transfers to Parnassus High School (New Kensington).
1925	Graduates from Parnassus; enters Pennsylvania College for Women (later named Chatham College).
1927	Changes her major from English to biology.
1929	Receives a bachelor of arts, magna cum laude, in biology; attends Marine Biological Laboratory at Woods Hole, Massachusetts, on a summer study fellowship. Enters Johns Hopkins University in the fall.
1930	Becomes teaching assistant at Johns Hopkins summer school (a job she holds through 1936). Carson's parents come to live with her in Maryland.
1931	Begins teaching at University of Maryland, College Park.
1932	Receives master of arts degree in marine zoology from Johns Hopkins.
1935	Father dies. Carson applies for a job at the U.S. Bureau of Fisheries; is hired temporarily to write radio scripts on marine life, then edit them for publication.
1936	Takes civil service examination, scores higher than any other examinee, and is given a full-time civil service ap-

pointment as junior aquatic biologist. Publishes nature and conservation articles in the *Baltimore Sun.*

1937   "Undersea" published in *Atlantic Monthly.* Carson's sister, Marian, dies, and Carson and her mother assume responsibility for Marian's daughters, Marjorie and Virginia Williams.

1941   *Under the Sea Wind,* based on "Undersea," published shortly before the Japanese attack on Pearl Harbor.

1942   Moves with family to Chicago, where she is assistant to the chief of the Office of Information in the Fish and Wildlife Service. Writes pamphlets encouraging Americans to eat fish.

1943   Returns to Washington.

1945   Suggests to *Reader's Digest* an article on DDT's effects on the natural world, which is rejected.

1945-1947   Named general editor of Conservation in Action, a series of pamphlets on wildlife refuges.

1948   Named editor-in-chief of Fish and Wildlife Information Division.

1949   Wins Eugene F. Saxton Memorial Fellowship to work on *The Sea around Us.*

1950   "Birth of An Island" (chapter from *The Sea around Us*) published in *Yale Review* and wins $1,000 Westinghouse award for best science writing in a magazine.

1951   *New Yorker* serial publication in June of excerpts from *The Sea around Us. The Sea around Us* published. Carson wins Guggenheim Fellowship to work on another book about the sea.

1952   First woman to receive the Henry G. Bryant Medal from the Philadelphia Geographical Society; receives honorary doctorates from Drexel Institute of Technology, Oberlin College, and Chatham College (her alma mater). *Under the Sea Wind* reissued. Resigns from the Fish and Wildlife Service to devote all her time to writing.

1955   *The Edge of the Sea* published. Begins children's book for her grandnephew, Roger, whom she adopts in 1957, after the death of his mother, Marjorie.

1956   Publishes "Help Your Child to Wonder," in *Women's Home Companion.*

1958   Carson agrees to write article for the *New Yorker* and a book for Houghton Mifflin on the subject of DDT and other toxic pesticides. Mother dies.

1962   *New Yorker* serial publication in June of excerpts from *Silent Spring. Silent Spring* published.

1963   "The Silent Spring of Rachel Carson" aired on CBS. President John F. Kennedy's Science Advisory Committee supports Carson's findings. Carson receives the National Audubon Society's medal and the American Geographical Society's medal, and is elected to the American Academy of Arts and Letters.

1964   Rachel Carson dies of cancer and heart failure.

1965   *A Sense of Wonder* published (reprint of "Help Your Child to Wonder"). Rachel Carson Council founded.

1969   Coastal Maine Wildlife Refuge renamed the Rachel Carson Natural Wildlife Refuge.

1980   Posthumously awarded President's Medal of Freedom.

1981   Rachel Carson stamp issued.

Chapter One

The Making of a Naturalist

Had Rachel Carson not written *Silent Spring* (1962) her biography would be simpler to write. The world would see her as a dedicated, literate marine biologist whose life and work was focused on the wonders of the sea. No one would have thought that this quiet woman, whose poetic passages in *Under the Sea Wind* (1941), *The Sea around Us* (1951), and *The Edge of the Sea* (1955) put her on the best-seller list for hundreds of weeks, was capable of generating the controversy that greeted the publication of her last book, *Silent Spring.*

Carson was always fascinated by the sea and by sea stories. Her interest in marine biology, her graduate thesis on catfish, her summer research at Woods Hole, her teaching assistantships in zoology labs at Johns Hopkins and the University of Maryland, and her job writing for the U. S. Bureau of Fisheries all set the stage for her writing about the sea. But what enabled her, a seemingly conventional, middle-aged woman, to confront the American scientific and business establishments and tell the world that we were destroying the planet we shared with other species? The answer to that question is that Carson's last book is not worlds apart from her earlier nature writing; it is the logical and integral conclusion to everything she did before. And it connects Carson with naturalists and conservationists writing both before and after she did.

Springdale

Springdale, Pennsylvania, approximately 18 miles from Pittsburgh on the Allegheny River, was a town of 1,199 people in 1910, when Rachel Carson was three; by 1920, the population had more than doubled.[1] It did have some industry, and during Carson's childhood a coal mining company tried to buy the mining rights under her father's land. Her father refused to sell those rights not only because the value of the land he hoped to sell as house lots would have been lowered but also because he did not trust the mine owners. He often suspected that they were tunneling and possibly mining underneath his property, ignoring his prohibition. While the Carsons still kept a horse and buggy, the automobile was coming to Springdale, as were streetcars, new businesses, and factories. Although the Carson property remained relatively rural and out of the bustle of the rapidly growing industry around Pittsburgh, changes were noticeable: the Allegheny valley was no longer the beautiful valley the first settlers had seen. Pittsburgh's industries had already destroyed much of the landscape not far from where Carson lived, and during the course of her childhood the ugliness moved closer to her home.

When she returned from college for the summer, before leaving for Woods Hole and then Johns Hopkins University to do graduate work, Carson noted that Springdale was no longer very pretty. Her father's acres were not as unspoiled as she remembered them from her woodlands walks with her parents, and the Allegheny River had become polluted by industrial waste. It was from this farewell to her childhood and its much-changed setting that Carson left home to view the ocean for the first time.

Early Years

Born 27 May 1907, Carson was the youngest of the three children of Maria McLean and Robert Warden Carson. Maria McLean Carson, the daughter of a Presbyterian minister, had studied classics at Washington Female Seminary, a Presbyterian school, and had taught before her marriage. She met Robert Carson when a church quartet, of which he was a member, came to town. Members of the United Presbyterian Church, Robert and Maria Carson continued to sing in the church choir, and Maria instilled in all her children a love of music. Eight years younger than her closest sibling, Robert, Carson had many advantages of an only child – a close relationship with her mother, a comfortable companionship with her siblings, and plenty of time on her own. Her mother, fearing the tendency toward illness in the family, often kept Carson out of school for long periods of time to avoid contagion when infectious diseases were in the area. Carson began Springdale Grammar School in 1913, but was only present "sixteen days in the first three months of the fall 1914 term" (Sterling, 16). Her spotty attendance throughout grade school would have failed a weaker student, but Carson's intelligence and her mother's encouragement helped her make up the lost time. When she wasn't at school, she was reading, writing, and developing a reverence for the world around her. The time she spent at home with her mother was rich with learning. The enforced absences from school, spent wandering in the orchards and woods, had a positive impact on Carson's development as a naturalist, an impact she was to recall in *A Sense of Wonder* (1965). In it, she takes her grandnephew, Roger Christie, out into the woods of Maine in much the same way that her mother took her into the woods of Springdale.

Carson's childhood was one that fostered a sense of herself and a sense of respect for the natural world. She often wandered in the family orchards looking for birds and other animals. She was unhappy with her brother's penchant for hunting rabbits and told him that, while he might enjoy it, "it can't be much fun for the rabbits" (Sterling, 20). Eventually, the gentle persuasions of the conservationist in the Carson family won out over the hunter, and Robert stopped. While this tale might be apocryphal, a part of family mythology, it reveals an interesting similarity with Henry David Thoreau's growing sense of shame at hunting and offers a window on the Carson family's sensitivity to the natural world.

Rachel was not the only one in her family who was sensitive to the creatures of the natural world. Her mother would not kill the insects that entered the house; rather, she would collect them and put them outside. Her father, while he would happily sell apples from his orchard for far less than the going rate, was always upset by people who would break the tree branches to get free fruit.

While not well off, the Carson family was land-rich. Robert Carson had bought 65 acres to sell as house lots and then added another 10 to that. Because he was unable to sell many of the lots, the Carsons always lived in what seemed to be a rural setting. They kept a pig, some chickens, and horses. Their house was outside Springdale, so Rachel spent a lot of time alone or with her mother. It was in many respects a self-sufficient and comfortable existence.

In this setting Carson began to write. She wrote poems and stories for her family, and at the age of 10 sent one to *St. Nicholas* magazine and won $10. She sent another story and won again.

Between September 1918 and August 1919, Carson won three prizes for her writing (Sterling, 27). This success fostered in her the idea that she could become a writer, an ambition that her mother encouraged. Carson set out to sell her stories, and when she was 14 or 15 sent a story entitled "Just Dogs" to readers at the Author's Press in Auburn, New York, requesting they read and send out her manuscript for publication. Like her later efforts to enter graduate school and the federal government, this early foray into publishing was both well organized and assertively handled.

After attending grammar school in Springdale, Carson attended two high schools – Springdale, a two-year school, and Parnassus High – where her hard work and intelligence earned her high grades. She was still writing, and her teachers encouraged her. It is not surprising that Carson decided to major in English at Pennsylvania College for Women in Pittsburgh (now Chatham College).

Pennsylvania College for Women

When Carson entered college in the fall of 1925, she was just 18, had never been away from home, and was financially strapped. She had graduated as one of the outstanding students in her high school class. Her enthusiasm for college life is expressed in an essay she wrote at the time, "Who I Am and Why I Came to PCW." In it she said she loved the outdoors, athletics, reading, and "the beautiful things of nature."[2] Carson admitted that she was no champion athlete, but nonetheless enjoyed swimming, tennis, hiking, riding, and basketball. She tried out for several sports teams. While usually not a first-string player, she did attend practices and was a substitute player for the basketball, baseball, and hockey teams (Sterling, 44). Eventually, she worked her way up to goalie on a winning hockey team. This athletic activity adds an unexpected dimension to the bookish Carson, and it shows the extent to which she threw herself into college life.

More important to her goal of becoming a writer than her participation in sports was her work for the *Arrow*, the school's semimonthly newspaper, and for the *Englicode*, the literary supplement to the paper. Throughout her college years, Carson wrote stories for the *Englicode*, among them, "Why I Am a Pessimist," "Keeping an Expense Account," and "The Golden Apple" (Sterling, 47). This last story reveals that Carson was beginning to be troubled by several issues that would determine her future. The story asks why women have to rely on men to make choices for them, as Paris is asked to choose who is the fairest woman. This poses a double problem for the women in the story: not only are they prevented from making their own decisions, but they must often submit their wills to men far less astute than they are.

Carson's observation of her mother's experience likely played some role in this story. She might well have looked back on her childhood in light of her experiences at college and asked why her mother's talents were channeled in such a limited sphere. Her father, who tried to combine farming and real estate, was not a successful businessman. His real estate schemes often came to nothing, and his attempts to deal with large companies, such as the coal mines, often proved unrewarding. Yet, in the tradition of the times, he made all the decisions. Maria Carson, whose father had died when she was 11, had seen her own mother flourish as a family provider, and she and her sister, Ida, worked to pay their way. Would family life and finances have been different had Maria Carson been able to make some of the choices?

Carson saw that her mother, a strong, talented woman who had received honors in Latin and who had much skill as a pianist, was totally dependent on a man who could not make money. Would her own dreams of writing be forfeited to the needs of a husband and family, and would her hopes be limited by someone less talented and intelligent than her? She might well have feared that her life would be constrained in the same way her mother's had been. Her mother had taught for a few years, but upon marrying had given up her work to take care of her family. Could Carson expect the same? Certainly, if she continued her study of literature, she could not anticipate making her living as a writer. She too might become a teacher, if only to pay off her college debts, and perhaps then marry and give up all hope of fulfilling her dreams. These concerns may have illuminated her telling of the story of Paris.

Another story written as a college theme sheds light on Carson's struggle to decide whether or not to change her major from English to biology. "Broken Lamps" tells of an engineer who wants nothing more than to build a beautiful bridge in which aesthetic perfection is blended with use. All his plans, however, reveal that his beautiful creation would not take the necessary stress. Depressed, he returns to more utilitarian models with the question, "God, could one not serve his soul and earn his bread?" He also thinks his wife looks upon him merely as a builder of bridges, "a man utterly incapable of appreciating the beautiful."[3] This short sketch highlights what might have concerned Carson at the time. Would becoming a scientist make it impossible for her to become a writer? Would others see her as insensitive to the beauty of the world she so relished? Would she end, as the engineer did, by giving up her aesthetic goals for purely utilitarian ones? All these questions were finally resolved when Carson decided, at the end of her sophomore year, to change her major and, as she told a fellow student, focus her writing on the world of science. Dorothy Thompson Seif remembers Carson's statement: "I have always wanted to write, but I don't have much imagination. Biology has given me something to write about. I will try in my writing to make animals in the woods or waters, where they live, as alive to others as they are to me."[4]

Biology Major

Most Carson biographers, as well as Carson herself, credit Mary Scott Skinker, who taught biology at Pennsylvania College, with the shift in the direction of Carson's life. In 1926, during her second year at Pennsylvania College for Women, Carson enrolled in biology to fulfill the two-semester science requirement. At year's end, much to the consternation of the English department and the college administration, which had given Carson scholarship money and encouraged her to become a writer, she switched her major to biology.

Carson saw in biology an opportunity to focus on a topic wholeheartedly. Her short stories for the *Englicode* reveal that Carson felt the need of a subject. Most women writers of the 1920s could expect to write for women's magazines on domestic matters: children, family, love, cooking – in short, home economics. Carson's interests clearly did not lie here. While she did not have the experience behind her to write stories like those by Herman Melville, Joseph Conrad, or Mark Twain (her favorite American author), she could as a scientist depict what she saw in the natural world she loved. Moreover, Carson's efforts at pure "literature" seem to have been unsuccessful. In *The House of Life: Rachel Carson at Work*, Paul Brooks, who was Carson's editor at Houghton Mifflin, notes that she sent verse to *Poetry, Atlantic Monthly, Good Housekeeping, Woman's Home Companion, Saturday Evening Post, Century Magazine, American Magazine, Delineator, Youth's Companion,* and other periodicals,[5] but her records show only rejections. "At the time," writes Brooks, Carson "believed that she had abandoned her dream of a literary career; only later did she realize that, on the contrary, she had discovered what she wanted to write about" (Brooks, 18). With the help of her mentor, Mary Skinker, Carson was taking the first step along a long road that would develop her true talent.

Skinker was surprised by Carson's decision, but her influence on her student was undeniable. A woman in a field dominated by men, she represented a life with larger possibilities than Carson's mother. Carson did not need to go back home, teach for a few years, then marry. Mary Skinker was returning to Johns Hopkins for her Ph.D. Carson might hope to do the same. If Maria Carson made it possible for her youngest daughter to go to college, Skinker made it possible for her to dream of more. In response to Skinker's encouragement, Carson and a few other science majors at the college started a science club, named Mu Sigma, or MS, after Mary Skinker. While Carson was seen as a quiet and unassertive member of her dormitory (a loner in the eyes of her more gregarious classmates) and while she was often unable to keep up with her more financially secure classmates, she became a leader in the science club; in her senior year Carson was elected president. She also formed a close personal friendship with Mary Skinker, who fostered in Carson the belief that she should continue her studies beyond college. H. Patricia Hynes sees the relationship between Skinker and Carson as part of a larger pattern to assure talented women a place in the scientific world. The teacher "would encourage her protégé and develop a close personal relationship. She would guide her selection of a graduate school; correspond with her and oversee her progress in graduate school; and when she was finishing, arrange a position for her in the college's department. The student would join her mentor on the faculty, taking over some of her responsibilities and freeing her for other interests" (Hynes, 60-61).

While this relationship was somewhat truncated by Skinker's failure to return to Pennsylvania College, she was able to advise Carson on graduate schools and always maintained an interest in her student's work. In the fall of 1928 Carson applied, with strong recommendations from Skinker, to Johns Hopkins University graduate school and was accepted as a student for the fall of 1929. She also won a place at the Marine Biological Laboratory at Woods Hole on Cape Cod for that summer, but first she had to graduate. She did so magna cum laude in the spring of 1929, and left Pennsylvania College with a sense of where her life was heading.

Carson grew in many ways during her years at college. She learned to manage away from the protective environment her mother had always provided despite financial hardship, and she got her first lesson in politics. When Carson was a junior, Mary Skinker took a leave of absence from the college to work on her Ph.D. at Johns Hopkins University in Maryland. Carson looked forward to her return, planning to take more courses with her during her senior year. But Skinker did not return. She became ill, could not attend Johns Hopkins, and instead went to Washington, D.C., to live with her sister.

Carson began to feel that there was a resistance on the part of the college to Skinker's return even after she recovered. This worried her because she found the other science teachers to be much less rigorous. During her senior year, Carson and a few of her friends, especially Mary Frye and Dorothy Thompson, found themselves at odds with the administration over the focus of the science programs at the college. The three young women all wanted to go to graduate school and had received quite a bit of encouragement and preparation from Skinker, but the administration wanted a less demanding program – one more suited to the needs of most students. Carson was angry at the college for its disregard of Skinker's influence on the best science students. President Cora Coolidge, whose relationship with Skinker had already been strained over the last year, felt that Carson and other members of Mu Sigma should not be criticizing the college. When they did, their relationship with the college also became strained. Skinker never did return to Pennsylvania. She continued her scientific research in parasitology for the U.S. Department of Agriculture and earned her doctorate at George Washington University.[6] It is ironic that Carson's first science mentor would work for the government agency that was later most negative in its assessment of her research on pesticides in the 1950s and early 1960s. The Department of Agriculture was in the vanguard of the attack against *Silent Spring*.

When Carson was working on that very difficult book, she would recall her conflict with Cora Coolidge and see again how different agendas determine the way people respond to the world. When she discussed her book with Clarence Cottam, a scientist who had just finished a study of the effectiveness of DDT against fire ants, he warned her that her facts would not necessarily convince the U.S. Department of Agriculture, which had a totally different agenda, about the dangers of pesticide use.

Woods Hole

In the summer of 1929, at the age of 22, Carson went to Woods Hole. She roomed with her friend and fellow Mu Sigma member, Mary Frye, who, like Carson, was there on a scholarship. The two women rented an inexpensive room in a widow's house and ate their meals at the Marine Biological Laboratory dining hall for only $7 a week (Sterling, 73). That summer, seeing the ocean for the first time in her life, Carson became a scientist.

Living on the ocean was a thrill for the young woman. While she spent a fair amount of time learning to swim, sunbathing, and writing enthusiastic letters to friends and family, she was completely immersed in studies that would focus her work at Johns Hopkins. She began to work on an original project on turtles that R. P. Cowles, her professor at Johns Hopkins, thought would be publishable (Sterling, 74). Unfortunately, she was not able to get the turtles she needed for the project, so her research was halted. During that idyllic summer, Carson saw living sea creatures for the first time and was continually enchanted by new discoveries. The vividness of these first impressions are evident in her books about the sea.

On her way to Woods Hole Carson had stopped in at Johns Hopkins to discuss her graduate program with Cowles. Carson had cultivated the habit of approaching people with whom she wished to work or from whom she needed information or assistance. She had contacted a writing service as a child to get help with publishing, and she had continued to seek out Skinker's advice after her teacher left Pennsylvania College. After leaving Woods Hole, on her way to Baltimore to begin her graduate program, she visited Elmer Higgins of the U.S. Bureau of Fisheries. Many researchers from the bureau were working at Woods Hole; through them she got an introduction to the man who was later to be her supervisor. She specifically wanted to know how she should prepare for a job as a marine biologist. She impressed him as articulate, curious, and knowledgeable, but he warned her that there were very few jobs for women scientists. A woman, he cautioned her, would never get a job in industry. She would have to depend on teaching or on government work. It was this same man who, after Carson had finished her master's degree, would open the door for her to full-time work.

Carson followed this pattern of seeking advice and of seeking out mentors all her life. Her search for an agent, which led to her lifelong working relationship with Marie Rodell, was conducted in the same methodical manner. Her correspondence with scientists when she was working on her three books about the sea reveals the same focused and organized approach, as do her research files on *Silent Spring*.

Johns Hopkins

Carson entered Johns Hopkins University early in October 1929. Within weeks, the country was plunged into the Great Depression. She was lucky to get a job as a teaching assistant in the Johns Hopkins summer school. Although she never had the luxury of being a nonworking graduate student and was still saddled with the worries of paying back loans to Pennsylvania College, her life at Johns Hopkins was not so fraught with the financial exigencies of her undergraduate years. During her second year at Johns Hopkins she supplemented her income by serving as Raymond Pearl's lab assistant. With her money concerns taken care of temporarily, Carson still had to find a suitable project for her master's thesis. Cowles suggested work with the temporary kidney of the channel catfish. Carson's project on the catfish involved meticulous preparation of slides, extensive study of the research done on the fish, and a thorough description of the development of the temporary kidney from day 2, when it begins to develop in the catfish egg, until day 11, when it has disappeared.

Throughout her second year at Johns Hopkins, Carson divided her time between her job as Pearl's assistant and her own research. At this time, to help with finances and to be with their daughter, her parents moved from Springdale to Stemmer's Run outside Baltimore on the Chesapeake Bay, and Carson commuted by train and bus every day to the university. While Carson herself had urged her parents to move to Baltimore to lessen the financial strain of keeping up two households, the added commute did cut into her work time. In the fall of 1931, when Carson was still working on her thesis, Cowles secured her a part-time teaching position at the University of Maryland in College Park. Her commute was lengthened. She went to College Park to teach, to Johns Hopkins to work on her research, and home to Stemmer's Run to be with her family. By spring 1932, when she was 25, Carson had finished her thesis and was awarded a master of arts in marine zoology (Sterling, 85), but she still did not have full-time employment as a scientist. She stayed on as a part-time teacher at the University of Maryland until December 1933, and from mid-1935 through 1936 worked only at Johns Hopkins summer school (Sterling, 86).

Perhaps Carson did not seek full-time work because she had just finished a grueling stint of research. Perhaps she felt uncertain about entering a male-dominated field; perhaps she just wanted time to decide how to use her degree. Or perhaps, as Margaret Rossiter suggests in *Women Scientists in America*, there were real obstacles to women seeking careers in the sciences.[7] Carson may have encountered these obstacles at Johns Hopkins and the University of Maryland. If a woman did not have a powerful mentor, she could not hope to get any position. Even if she did have a male on the faculty who supported her research and gave her assistantships and lectureships, her chances of becoming anything more than an assistant professor were slim. The prejudice against women in academic science departments was so intense that even the most brilliant female protégés of prestigious male scientists were often passed over for promotion despite their mentor's support. Indeed, the common prejudice that "no good job should ever be wasted on a woman" (Rossiter, 91) was very real in Carson's world. In addition, the Depression limited the number of jobs available and further heightened the prejudice against hiring women when good young men were out of work.

Cowles, who helped Carson with her research at Johns Hopkins and whom Carson often looked to for guidance and mentoring, did help Carson get a part-time job at the University of Maryland. It is hard to imagine him writing a similar recommendation for a male protégé, however. Sterling quotes his letter to Professor C. J. Pierson, hastily dashed off in pencil: "Miss Carson is a young lady of excellent character. She is pleasing in appearance and capable in everything she does. Her scholarship has been high in her undergraduate studies and also in her graduate work here" (Sterling, 84-85). The only "excellent" Cowles gives Carson is in character, and he places character and appearance before her ability. His letter indicates only a hard-working young woman who needs a job.

Whatever Carson's problems were with finding a job in her chosen field, the death of her father in the summer of 1935 and the divorce of her sister, Marian, who with her two daughters came to live with Carson and her mother, increased Carson's financial obligations and forced her to look for full-time employment outside of academia. She turned to Elmer Higgins, now head of the Division of Scientific Inquiry at the Bureau of Fisheries, who in the fall of 1929 had warned her about the lack of scientific positions for women and indicated that government work would likely be one of the few options open to her.

Government Employment

As it turned out, professional positions for women in government, as elsewhere, were almost nonexistent. Carson was to become only the second woman hired by the U.S. Bureau of Fisheries for a nonsecretarial post. Fortunately for Carson, Higgins had just been commissioned to do a series of radio broadcasts on marine life. After a brief interview, though he'd seen nothing Carson had written, he decided to give her a chance. He asked if she'd be interested in writing some of the scripts. Higgins was pleased with Carson's first efforts and determined to keep her on the project, paying her $19.25 a week. When the broadcasts were finished, he asked her to edit the material for government publication.

Carson was lucky to be at the bureau in 1936 when the civil service examination for a position as junior aquatic biologist was posted in the office where she worked. Had she not been working there, she would most likely never have heard of the opening. As it was, she was the only woman to sit for the exam. She received the highest score and the position. Her salary immediately doubled.

At the bureau, Higgins served as her mentor; he recognized her talents and gave her good advice about her writing. Of the piece she wrote to introduce the newly edited essays she had originally put together for radio production, he commented that it was far too good for publication in a government pamphlet. It deserved separate publication, and he suggested she try the *Atlantic*. Eventually Carson took Higgins's advice, and the *Atlantic* published the piece as "Undersea" in September 1937. Higgins then suggested that she expand the article into a book. What he saw in Carson was a meticulous scientist who was also a gifted writer. He helped Carson to focus on the possibilities of writing about the sea and its creatures. Again Carson took Higgins's advice, and *Under the Sea Wind* was published in 1941, just before the Japanese invasion of Pearl Harbor brought America into World War II.

Carson worked for the Bureau of Fisheries – and its incarnation since 1940, the Fish and Wildlife Service – from 1935 until 1952. For the most part she lived in Silver Spring, Maryland, but for a few months during the war she lived in Chicago; her office had been transferred there because the government needed space in Washington for the war effort. While in Chicago, Carson wrote pamphlets to convince Americans to eat more fish. During her government service she also worked on her own projects. She regularly published articles in the *Baltimore Sun* and worked on *Under the Sea Wind* and *The Sea around Us*.

Carson was rewarded for her competence as a scientist with fairly regular promotions: from 1942 to 1943 she was an assistant aquatic biologist; from 1943 to 1945, an associate aquatic biologist; and from 1945 to 1946, an aquatic biologist. (It is noteworthy that even as recently as 1992, almost 30 years after the publication of *Silent Spring*, her credentials were misrepresented. An article in the *New York Times Book Review* on important books written by women in the 1960s recognized *Silent Spring* as a "seminal" book on the environment, but claimed that its author "was not a scientist of any kind."[8] This misleading view has dogged the research on her life and work.)

In spite of this steady stream of promotions, Carson attempted to leave government service around the mid-1940s. She was not making much money, even though she was able to supplement her salary by regularly publishing magazine articles. After the war she applied for several jobs that she felt would better suit her interests and give her more time to write. She sought work at the New York Zoological Society, but even with a critically and scientifically acclaimed book, she was rejected. She also sought a position with the National Audubon Society, but was not accepted. Given her experience and credentials, this turn of events seems to indicate that the problems she encountered during the Depression were at work once again. Men were returning from World War II and were being given preference. Further, Higgins's warning back in 1929 that it would be hard for a female scientist to secure challenging work still held true in the 1940s.

Her unfruitful search for work outside the Fish and Wildlife Service led her to refocus her attention on the writing she was doing within it, and her last two government positions reflected this. From 1946 to 1949 Carson worked as information specialist at the service, and from 1949 to 1952, when she left government service, served as editor-in-chief of its Information Division. While in these positions she organized a well-respected series of pamphlets on American wildlife refuges entitled Conservation in Action, researching and writing a number of the pamphlets herself. Carson's writings outside of her work for the government were also gaining an audience. *Colliers* magazine accepted a piece she wrote on bat radar, "The Bat Knew It First,"⁹ and paid her $500. The navy also used the piece because of its clear introduction to radar.

At about this time Carson attempted an interesting project that is rarely reported in standard biographical material about her. Several paintings of birds by Louis Agassiz Fuertes hung in the offices of the Fish and Wildlife Service. Carson conceived the idea of writing a text to accompany the paintings and hoped to convince her editor at Oxford University Press, Paul Vaudrin, to publish it alongside reproductions of the paintings. She wrote of her plans to her agent, Marie Rodell, and in 1949 began a correspondence with Mary Fuertes Boynton, the painter's daughter, to get permission to do the text. At first, Boynton seemed happy with Carson's proposal, but as the correspondence continued Boynton began placing obstacles in the way, ultimately rejecting Carson's proposal, ostensibly because she wanted a writer with more expertise in the field of ornithology. Carson, who had been completely open about her plans for the project, who had a critically acclaimed book, *Under the Sea Wind,* to her credit, and who had written extensively about birds for the Conservation in Action series, felt betrayed; her memos to others in the Fish and Wildlife Service indicate how disappointed she was by the project's ultimate failure (Beinecke papers). Had Boynton accepted Carson's credentials as a writer and a scientist, future generations would have gotten to know her father's work much better; Boynton never did publish such a book.

Carson's various creative and professional disappointments aside, she worked hard and elicited great loyalty from the people who worked for her in the Fish and Wildlife Service. A story told by Bob Hines, a wildlife artist who later became Carson's friend and the illustrator for *The Edge of the Sea,* indicates this. It also shows the upward battle Carson likely had throughout her career in government because she was female. "I had just been hired as an artist for the U.S. Fish and Wildlife Service," Hines writes. "When I was offered the job, I had been told I'd be supervised by a woman, and having done odd jobs for hard-to-please-housewives during the Depression, I was apprehensive."[10] Hines even considered turning down the job. After his initial misgivings, Hines began to see Carson's strengths as a supervisor and described her managerial style: "She knew how to get things done the quickest, simplest, most direct way. . . . She didn't like shoddy work or shoddy behavior. She was just so doggone good she couldn't see why other people couldn't try to be the same. She had standards, high ones" (Sterling, 111).

While her primary responsibilities at the Bureau of Fisheries and at the Fish and Wildlife Service were writing, editing, and producing the documents put out by the information division, her scientific expertise and thoroughness gave her credibility with the many scientists she had to work with. She once pointed out to Bob Hines that he had put one spine too many in the dorsal fin of a mullet he had drawn (Sterling, 112).

Family and Friends

Both Paul Brooks, Carson's editor at Houghton Mifflin, and Shirley Briggs, her longtime friend and coworker at the Fish and Wildlife

Service, claim that Carson's life was her work and that any biography must focus primarily on her work. But there were relationships that Carson valued that influenced her work and gave shape to her life. In a college theme, "Friendship," written in 1925, Carson wrote that friendship should be considered a sacred trust that improves the character and intellectual standards of both people in the relationship (Beinecke papers). That concept of friendship was Carson's guide throughout her life.

Clearly her mother had an enormous impact on Carson. Except for the four years she spent at Pennsylvania College and her first year at Johns Hopkins, Carson and her mother lived together until the latter's death in 1958. But the Carson household included not just the two. At Maria Carson's urging, they kept Marian Carson Williams's daughters, Marjorie and Virginia, when Carson's older sister died at the age of 40 in 1937. Before Carson was 30, she was financially responsible for the household. While Carson worked, Maria Carson made a home for her daughter and her granddaughters. This home life was extremely important to Carson, for it both grounded her and freed her.

H. Patricia Hynes, author of *The Recurring Silent Spring*, takes Carson's male biographers to task for trying to explain the fact that Carson never married. In *The House of Life*, Paul Brooks writes that Carson was prevented by her failure to marry "from enjoying what Thoreau called a broad margin to her life" (Brooks, 242). What so marks that statement as narrow is the assumption that Carson's life, as rich as it was with work, family, and friends, was incomplete because she did not marry. Had she married during the Depression or just after her life might have been diminished. She might have become the self-sacrificing wife her mother became.

In fact, some blame for Carson's failure to marry has been placed on her mother. "It is probably an understatement to say that Maria Carson never urged Rachel to marry," Brooks writes (242). Whatever her mother's influence, given narrow roles prescribed for most wives and mothers at the time, Carson may well have been better able to follow the true path of her talent as a single woman. Carson's role in her household was like that of an older sister. This role gave her companionship when she wanted it and freedom and privacy when she needed it. Further, the fact that Carson was the breadwinner gave her power within the family structure that she could not have achieved as a wife. It was not a power she wielded autocratically, but it gave her a sense of self that she might never have achieved in a traditional marriage.

The depth of the relationship between Carson and her mother is elegized in a letter Carson wrote to Marjorie Spock on 4 December 1958, after Maria Carson died, while Carson herself was battling cancer and working on *Silent Spring:* "Her love of life and of all living things was her outstanding quality, of which everyone speaks. More than anyone else I know, she embodied Albert Schweitzer's 'reverence for life,' and while gentle and compassionate, she could fight fiercely against anything she believed wrong, as in our present Crusade! Knowing how she felt about that will help me return to it soon, and to carry it through to completion" (Beinecke papers).

Both Hynes and Briggs criticize Brooks for diminishing, in his biography, the margins of Carson's life. Hynes points out that Thoreau, whose phrase Brooks uses to fault Carson's, was himself not married and yet was someone whom Brooks presumably thinks did, indeed, have broad margins to his life. If Thoreau's life was broad, says Briggs, so was Carson's: "If anyone lived [life] at the broad margins it was she" (Hynes, 66). Moreover, if any one thing could be said to have narrowed her life, it would have to be her government work. Like Thoreau, she keenly felt the imprisonment of having to mortgage her life to a daily job.

After her mother, it was probably Mary Scott Skinker who most radically changed the direction of Carson's life. Over the years Carson remembered Skinker's help, and while they did not see each other often after Skinker left Washington to teach in Chicago, Carson did visit her, at great personal expense, when she was suffering from cancer, prior to her death in 1950.

Marie Rodell was also a valued friend. Carson selected Rodell as her agent after careful consideration and several interviews. Did Carson consciously seek out a female agent? Hynes believes she did, a choice in keeping with Carson's lifelong valuing of women (Hynes, 11). Others doubt that gender played a role in Carson's choice. In any case, she clearly would have wanted a capable professional with whom she felt comfortable. After giving Rodell an outline and sample chapter of *The Sea around Us*, which a publisher could not commit itself to at the time, Carson found herself comforting her agent rather than vice versa, and the two women became close friends.

In 1949, soon after Carson chose Rodell as her agent, both women found themselves together on the *Albatross III,* a converted trawler stationed at Woods Hole. The Fish and Wildlife Service was investigating the scarcity of valuable commercial fish on Georges Bank, the rich fishing grounds off the Massachusetts coast, so Carson decided to combine work for the service with research on *The Sea around Us.* The *Albatross* had never taken women out before, and the crew felt that one woman would pose problems. Two women were deemed acceptable, so Carson asked Rodell to accompany her. Rodell recorded the experience in a diary, which reveals how the women were initiated into the life on the ship. "The third mate filled up our ears with horror stories," she writes. " 'Always hang on to something,' he warned us; 'the water coming over the decks can bang you about a lot.' From the wheelhouse, he pointed down to an open hatch in the center of the forward deck; we could see a spindly ladder leading down. 'That's where you eat,' he said and bowed us off the ship with sadistic pleasure" (Brooks, 115).

Rodell proved tireless in her efforts to promote Carson's work. She sent out chapters of *The Sea around Us* to magazine after magazine. Finally, in 1949, the *Yale Review* accepted "The Birth of An Island," which won Carson the George Westinghouse Science Writing Award. After the *New Yorker* accepted several chapters, acceptances began to mount for portions of the book. Marie Rodell's persistence paid off financially for Carson at a time when she really needed it.

The compatibility of author and agent is further illustrated in their shared dislike of the Hollywood production of *The Sea around Us.* Both felt that it was a nightmare of scientific errors. Ironically, despite the author's disapproval, the film won an Oscar for best documentary for 1953.

When toward the end of her life Carson was confined to a wheelchair but still determined to carry out her speaking schedule, it was Marie Rodell who accompanied her. The choice of an agent had been for both Carson and Rodell a richly rewarding personal and intellectual venture that lasted almost two decades.

Another valued friend was Shirley Briggs. She and Carson both worked at the Fish and Wildlife Service and enjoyed bird-watching. They joined the Audubon Naturalist Society of the Central Atlantic States and, during the war, were able to bird-watch with such experienced birders as Roger Tory Peterson, who had been called to Washington on wartime assignment. Briggs also worked with Carson on the Conservation in Action series.

An illustration of the broad range of Carson's friendships is revealed in her correspondence with Beverly Knecht from 1958 to 1959. In 1958 Knecht wrote to Carson about *The Edge of the Sea*. Knecht had become blind in her senior year in college and was in the hospital at the time she wrote to Carson. Sympathetic to the frustration of the former art major, Carson encouraged her to write. She often stopped to visit Knecht when driving to or from her home in Maine and encouraged her reading. Carson made notes in the margins of Beverly's letters so she could answer her queries and comments specifically. What is significant about this correspondence is that Carson, normally described as shy and reserved, showed such warmth and generosity to Beverly Knecht.

With the enormous success of *The Sea around Us* in 1951 and the reissue of *Under the Sea Wind* in 1952, Carson was able to leave her job at the Fish and Wildlife Service and devote her time to writing. She was also able to fulfill a long-held dream of a cottage on the Maine coast. She bought a one-and-a-half acre lot at West Southport and began to plan the cottage. It would have windows all around, so she could view the ocean and the sky. She also found lasting friends in Maine. Dorothy and Stanley Freeman, who had a cottage less than a mile down the coast, were admirers of *The Sea around Us* and wrote to Carson when they found out she was building a house near theirs. That letter began a friendship that would last 10 years, until Carson's death in 1964. It was the Freemans who showed Carson many caves and tide pools that were invaluable to her research for *The Edge of the Sea*. Dorothy Freeman was also a close friend during Carson's last illness, spending many hours walking in Maine's Newegan refuge with her in the summer of 1963. The companionship of Dorothy Freeman made the last years of Carson's life richer.

Colleagues

Carson's government work and her writing brought her a range of professional colleagues whose support, especially during the furor that developed in the early 1960s over *Silent Spring*, was invaluable.

Elmer Higgins of the Fish and Wildlife Service, to whom Carson often
referred as her first literary agent for his encouragement and advice
on writing early in her career, shared many of Carson's views on the
balance of nature. In the 1950s he had written about the possible
negative, long-term effects of DDT on the quality of human life. His
position, when government and industry were working closely to
produce and use more and more pesticides, was a real support to
Carson. Another colleague who supported Carson's findings on DDT
was Clarence Cottam. A highly regarded scientist, Cottam had
worked with Carson at the Fish and Wildlife Service on the
Conservation in Action pamphlets. He warned Carson that, while his
own research supported her findings on the effects of DDT on the
food chain, those groups with an interest in pesticide use would be
likely to attack her. Cottam had reason to warn her. When
investigating the Department of Agriculture's fire ant program he
found that the department, enamored with the quick-fix rhetoric of
the pesticide industries, had manipulated much of the data about
pesticides to support its policy on their use. A third supportive
government colleague was Bob Hines.

The publication of "Undersea" in September 1937 brought Carson into contact with a number of scientists and editors who were
interested in her investigation of the sea. Author and journalist
Henrik Willem van Loon, who wrote *The Story of Mankind,* was so
impressed with Carson's article that he spoke to Quincy Howe, his
editor at Simon and Schuster, who then wrote to Carson. It was from
this interest that Carson gained the confidence to begin her first
book. She credited van Loon with giving her frequent advice and
encouragement during the long process of writing *Under the Sea
Wind.*

Another valuable professional relationship for Carson was that
with William Beebe, the eminent marine biologist who recognized in
Carson's first book impeccable scientific accuracy. Beebe had
encouraged her to apply and recommended her for the position at
the New York Zoological Society, though to no avail. More important, he anthologized several chapters of *Under the Sea Wind* in his
anthology, *Book of Naturalists* (1944). It was also Beebe who
encouraged Carson to dive underwater to get a feel for the research
she was doing for *The Sea around Us.* No one could write genuinely
about the sea, he believed, without going in it.

Another naturalist and writer sympathetic to Carson's cosmology was Edwin Way Teale. His *Grassroot Jungles* was published in 1937, the same year as Carson's "Undersea," and the two developed a correspondence that spanned decades. It was Carson who in 1956 advised Teale to get an advance sampling of his *Autumn across America* in two magazines before its release to bookstores in order to improve sales. The two also helped each other with research. Carson elicited his help in a letter, dated 12 October 1958, asking for information on the decline of bird populations for *Silent Spring*. She wanted "factual comparisons that will hold up under fire" (Beinecke papers).

Paul Brooks, Carson's editor for *The Sea around Us, The Edge of the Sea,* and *Silent Spring,* revived public interest in Carson in the early 1970s with his *House of Life,* a biography of Carson at work. Unlike the relationship Carson had with her agent, her relationship with her editor, though friendly and respectful, was not intimate. There is in Brooks's account a recognition of the enormous impact that her three books about the sea and crusading text about pesticides had on our general understanding of the natural world.

Years after Carson's death, Louis J. Halle, a naturalist and writer who had also worked for the State Department, said of Carson that she lived an "authentic life." The phrase bespeaks Carson's genuine commitment to her two loves: writing and science. She did indeed live fully and richly through them.

Chapter Two

First Voyage

"Undersea"

Rachel Carson, a child of a landlocked state who did not see the ocean until she graduated from college, said that the sea had fascinated her since she heard its sound mimicked in a decorative shell as a girl. In an autobiographical sketch, she says, "Among my earliest memories . . . are two things: a feeling of absolute fascination for every thing relating to the ocean, and a determination that I would someday be a writer" (Beinecke papers). "Undersea," published by the *Atlantic* in September 1937, is much like that shell: small, perfect, and hinting at a larger world. The article opens, "Who has known the ocean?" It then asks readers to shed their "human perceptions of length and breadth and time and place"[1] to enter a space that will utterly change their perspective on their world. Trapped on the land, human beings see little of what nature has created. "Undersea" was Carson's first attempt to help people see beyond the limits of their landlocked experience.

But the article did not simply illuminate aspects of the ocean; rather, it set up a clear cosmology that was to stay with Carson throughout her life. In it she began to weave the web that was to link all creatures of the earth into one harmonious and mutually necessary existence. The sense of connectedness that pervades the article foreshadows the guiding principle of all her later works. What she saw in nature, she imitated in her art. In the last paragraph of "Undersea" is the kernel of all her books about the sea:

> Thus we see the parts of the plan fall into place: the water receiving from earth and air the simple materials, storing them up until the gathering energy of the spring sun wakens the sleeping plants to a burst of dynamic activity, hungry swarms of planktonic animals growing and multiplying upon the abundant plants, and themselves falling prey to the shoals of

fish; all, in the end, to be redissolved into their component substances
when the inexorable laws of the sea demand it. Individual elements are
lost to view, only to reappear again and again in different incarnations in a
kind of material immortality. Kindred forces to those which, in some
period inconceivably remote, gave birth to that primeval bit of protoplasm
tossing on the ancient seas, continue their mighty and incomprehensible
work. ("Undersea," 29)

Carson's precise blending of form and content in her first major
magazine article gives an indication of how her writing would
develop, all the way to *Silent Spring*.

"Undersea" contains her introduction to tide pools, "seas in
miniature," which illustrate the way numberless plants and animals
live with and off each other: "sponges of the simpler kinds encrust
the rocks, each hungrily drawing in through its myriad mouths the
nutriment-laden water. . . . Shell-less cousins of the snail, the naked
sea slugs are spots of brilliant rose and bronze, spreading arbores-
cent gills to the waters, while the tube worms, architects of the tide
pools, fashion conical dwellings of sand grains, cemented one
against another in glistening mosaic" ("Undersea," 23-24). The
meticulous attention to the details of the pools not only illustrates
their importance for Carson in the pattern she saw in the interconnectedness of all parts of the ocean but also presages her much more
intense scrutiny of the pools in *The Edge of the Sea*.

Carson then turns to the seabirds who will figure prominently in
Under the Sea Wind. In "Undersea" they are nameless; nonetheless,
they are a vital part of the great chain of life that makes up the sea.
The birds rush in with the outgoing waves to capture their dinner in
the few seconds that the sand is bare. Then they must fly or run not
to be caught by the incoming tide.

Finally, Carson focuses on the sea itself, filled with vast ocean
pastures, great white sharks, the blue whale, and "living things so
small that your two hands might scoop up as many of them as there
are stars in the Milky Way" ("Undersea," 24).

"Undersea" shows Carson's awareness of how difficult it is for
people to visualize the sea. Many of her references to "ocean pastures," "rotund hedgehogs," and the "Milky Way" help the reader
find a point of reference in the ever fluent ocean. Eventually, however, there are no maps for the depths of the ocean: "In these silent

deeps a glacial cold prevails, a bleak iciness which never varies, summer or winter, years melting into centuries, and centuries into ages of geologic time. There too, darkness reigns – the blackness of primeval night in which the ocean came into being, unbroken, through eons of succeeding time, by the gray light of dawn" ("Undersea," 26).

Despite her sense of the place of everything in the sea, Carson does not pretend that the sea is a peaceful domain. "The sea is not a solicitous foster mother," she realizes. Plants live to become the food of animals which in turn are preyed upon by larger and larger animals. This food chain creates a balance in which every plant and animal has a function, and "every living thing of the ocean, plant and animal alike, returns to the water at the end of its own life span the materials that had been temporarily assembled to form its body" ("Undersea," 27). That sense of purpose and place in nature is central to Carson's philosophy; it is evident in her first major publication and her last public speech, given in the year she died.

Under the Sea Wind

That *Under the Sea Wind* grew organically out of "Undersea" is evident from the organization of the book, as Carson, acting on Elmer Higgins's suggestion, turned each section of the article into a part of the book. Book 1 deals with the "Edge of the Sea"; book 2, "The Gull's Way," focuses on the migratory patterns of birds and fish; book 3, "River and Sea," follows a female eel from its home in the river back to its birth and spawning place in the deepest ocean. Carson decided early how she would approach her subject, writing to Henrik van Loon on 5 February 1938 that "the entire book must be written in narrative form. . . . The fish and the other creatures must be the central characters and their world must be portrayed as it looks and feels to them . . . nor must any humans come into it except from the fishes' viewpoint as a predator and destroyer" (Beinecke papers).

The book is, in fact, a narrative of the lives of birds and fish as they travel in their peculiar migratory patterns. Driven by instincts that scientists have yet to understand fully, the animals of the sea and air are locked in timeless rituals that have the sea as their stage. Carson said in the foreword to the 1941 edition that "the sense of the sea, holding the power of life and death over every one of its creatures from the smallest to the largest, would inevitably pervade every page."[2] It is this sense that gives Carson's science mythic proportions in her three books about the sea.

Book 1: "Edge of the Sea"

Under the Sea Wind opens not in the ocean itself, but on an island off the coast of North Carolina where migrating black skimmers have settled for a brief period. One bird, Rynchops, creates the central point of view for the chapter. "Rynchops" is in fact the actual scientific name for the black skimmer; thus Carson at once particularizes the bird for her readers and locates him in the scientific lexicon. He becomes "the bird," all black skimmers, while retaining his particular identity. Rynchops's flights over the island reveal a pattern of life and death on land and sea. There is not hierarchy but rather an interdependence of all the creatures on the island and in the surrounding ocean.

This first chapter illustrates the activity of one night in early spring, but that activity also represents nature's timeless pattern of birth and death. It is flood tide on the island, and Carson describes the scene in a way that diminishes the difference between sea and land: "Both water and sand were the color of steel overlaid with the sheen of silver, so that it was hard to say where water ended and land began."[3]

Rynchops and the rest of the black skimmers have migrated from the Yucatan and will lay their eggs and hatch their young before returning south. The skimmers, or flood gulls, feed on the rising tide, and this gives Carson the opportunity to describe in vivid detail the cycles of feeding and flight that are so much a part of Rynchops's instinctive behavior.

The cycle of birth and death, eating and being eaten, sets the cyclic pattern for the first chapter and for the whole book. Even the eels, who are central to book 3 in their great migration to the ocean, are present in the opening chapter. The endless cycles described by Carson relate all creatures in the community of nature and connect them to its timeless patterns. The turtle lays its eggs on the sand and returns to the ocean, the swamp rat finds the eggs and begins to feast, but, intent on his dinner, does not notice the blue heron, which then eats him.

Life quickens at night when the shad begin to run, returning to their birthplace to spawn. Fishermen may catch the shad in their gill, or seine, nets, but the eels who live in the estuaries pick the shad bones clean, so that the nets are brought to the surface almost empty.

Nature has accounted for the terrible toll the nets and other predators take on the shad, with each roe fish laying hundreds of thousands of eggs. "Perhaps only one or two young would survive the perils of river and sea and return in time to spawn," Carson writes, "for by such ruthless selection the species are kept in check" (*USW*, 18).

There is a tooth-and-claw element to the opening chapters of *Under the Sea Wind*, but for Carson the cycles of predator and prey are part of a much grander cycle that is essentially harmonious. It is seeing the larger harmony that makes equanimity possible in the face of smaller violences. Carson sees beyond particular instances of destruction to create an almost instinctual, or at least archetypal, response to the sea, making it not simply the object of commercial or scientific interest but a poetic center.

The remainder of book 1, chapters 2-5, follows Blackfoot and Silverbar, two sanderlings, on their migration from South America to their nesting grounds in the Arctic. Blackfoot has made the journey several times, but his mate, Silverbar, is a yearling who is making the arduous journey for the first time. In this migration, Carson is able to show the integral relation of continents, oceans, and living creatures.

Central to the first book of *Under the Sea Wind* is the Arctic storm, which occurs in chapter 3, after the sanderlings arrive at their nesting grounds. The storm illustrates the delicate balance and constant shifting of the natural world. Carson does not romanticize nature; rather, she shows the interconnection of all the species on the tundra. The raging storm has caught the animals by surprise, and one, the snowy owl, abandons her nest and eggs to survive. Carson describes the death of the owl eggs: "The life fires of the tiny embryos burned low. . . . The pulsating red sacs under the great oversized heads hesitated, beat spasmodically, and were stilled. The six little owls-to-be were dead in the snow, and by their death, perhaps, hundreds of unborn lemmings and ptarmigans and Arctic hares had the greater chance of escaping death from the feathered ones that strike from the sky" (*USW*, 51-52).

Throughout book 1 Carson is concerned with how seemingly disparate elements are bound together. We can see clearly the processes that Carson finds so enduring: "For in the sea, nothing is lost. One dies, another lives, as the precious elements of life are passed on and on in endless chains" (*USW*, 105).

Book 2: "The Gull's Way"

The harmony of life and death, the connectedness of all parts of the ocean and the land, birds, fish, and plants is disturbed by human beings. The seine netting of the shad is an example of a small disruption; but the fisherman are, ironically, bested by the eels, who steal the catch. Another, more serious intrusion occurs midway through book 2. Trawlers have discovered the deep-water wintering grounds of the mackerel, halibut, haddock, and cod and have invaded the deep ocean space with their expansive nets. "Something vast and dark like a fish of monstrous and incredible size, its whole forward end a vast, gaping mouth, loomed in the water" (*USW*, 174). The fish respond instinctively; they hurry toward the edge of the abyss to seek safety in the dark waters, yet the trawl follows them into the once-safe depths. The trawl net, unlike nature itself, is indiscriminate in its catch. It "had already scooped up in its cavernous bag thousands of pounds of food fish, as well as quantities of basket starfish, prawns, crabs, clams, cockles, sea cucumbers, and white worm tubes" (*USW*, 174).

What Carson sees in the human incursions into the once-safe areas of the sea is chaos. The finely balanced cycles of birth, life, and death, preying and being preyed upon, are upset by the monstrous catches of the trawl nets. In book 1, the gill nets take many shad, but other sea creatures also benefit. The hungry eels are fed, and the gulls grab the fishheads as the fishermen toss them away. Trawlers with vast nets deplete the ocean bottoms where fish go to mature; not only do they kill countless sea creatures, but they kill them before they have a chance to spawn, and future generations are threatened as well. That, for Carson, who studied the depleted waters of Georges Bank for the Fish and Wildlife Service, was the greatest disruption resulting from the human quest for food. That same disruption of the balance of the natural world impelled Carson to write *Silent Spring;* she found that pesticides, intended to safe-guard food crops, not only prevented certain animals from repro-ducing but often mutilated the offspring of those who could.

Despite the interference of the trawlers with the life cycle of many fish, book 2 is the most unified of the three books of *Under the Sea Wind.* As in book 1, the narrative follows a central protagonist (if a fish can be called that) from his precarious birth in the waters off Long Island to his days as a yearling fish as he swims instinctively to "the deep quiet waters along the continental shelf, off the Cape of Virginia" (*USW*, 206). Scomber's name, like that of Rynchops, is the scientific name for his species – the mackerel. Like Rynchops's life, Scomber's is dominated by "the old, unchanging cycle of the sea" (*USW*, 110).

In her notebooks[4] for *Under the Sea Wind*, Carson outlines the life cycle of Scomber: "Birth of Scomber the mackerel, off New York – drift of water to south – increase of enemies and decrease of food – great decimater of numbers – return to New England waters when able to swim independently, attack of squid on young mack-erel." This outline intensifies the dramatic life of the mackerel. Car-son added to that note another which said, "must give feeling of sea nursery in which all kinds of young besides mackerel are develop-ing" (Beinecke papers).

Carson is able, in the book, to actualize her sense of the need for dramatic characters to illustrate the cycles of the sea. As an infant fish, Scomber can do nothing but float "where the sea carried him, now a rightful member of the drifting community of the plankton" (*USW*, 127). Many of his fellows did not survive; "thousands went no farther than the first stages of the journey into life until they were seized and eaten by the comb jellies, to be speedily converted into the watery tissue of their foe and in this reincarnation to roam the sea, preying on their own kind" (*USW*, 120). In these passages, Car-son heightens not only the dramatic presentation of the scientific information but also the sense of the connectedness of all creatures in the ocean. All play a role in an ordered scheme.

In the central chapter in book 2, "The Harbor," Carson brings Scomber to a protected New England harbor. There he spends the summer before returning to the deep waters to spawn. Carson's ability to present scientific information in a style that appeals to non-scientists is most apparent in this chapter. In her notebooks on

Under the Sea Wind Carson expresses her concern for what level of
reader she should address and how she could present scientific
information with both accuracy and drama. She questioned her editors about both matters and found that if she were able to become
the characters in the book, she could make the information both
interesting and accurate. In an undated memo to a Mrs. Eales, Carson states that most books about the sea "are written from the viewpoint of the human observer" and thus the reader has a difficult time
entering the world of the ocean. In writing *Under the Sea Wind,* Carson continues, "I was successively a sandpiper, a crab, a mackerel,
an eel and half a dozen other animals" (Beinecke papers). This ability to enter into the life of the creatures of the sea is abundantly
apparent in "The Harbor." Scomber grows and begins to hunt. Seeing herring fleeing a young pollock in terror, "a new instinct stirred
swiftly to life in the young mackerel. He swerved, banked steeply,
and seized a young herring athwart its body" (*USW,* 144). Scomber
has become a part of the chain of the hunter and the hunted.

The southwestern storm that brought the jellyfish into the harbor to die also heralds the change of the season, and Scomber, along
with the other young mackerel, is stirred to "a strange uneasiness."
He and his school, who have spent the summer in the relative quiet

of the harbor, "were carried in a swift rush of water past the rocks of the harbor mouth." They spend the rest of their lives in the open ocean (*USW*, 160).

In her memo to Eales, Carson said of the writing of *Under the Sea Wind*, "I very soon realized that the central character of the book was the ocean itself" (Beinecke papers). It was that growing realization that the book was really held together by each creature's relationship to the ocean that informs the entire text. The movement of the fish influences the migrations of birds, and all are held in the cycles of the tides and the seasons. Scomber's voyage to the deep ocean illustrates the power of the sea.

In depicting Scomber's journey with his mackerel school, Carson uses another device that once again puts all species in perspective in relation to one another. Using the vantage point of the gull, Carson is able to look down on the ocean and see the great variety of light and shadow, the many activities of the sea creatures. The panoramic effect of the scene clearly defines the connection of all species in the food chain. The gull, hanging above the water, notices two schools of mackerel, old and young, merge, cross each other's paths, and separate. Then the gulls see the two dark fins of the swordfish resting near the surface in wait for the rich schools of plankton that will bring other food fish to his vicinity. The gull also notices a great disturbance in the water as shrimp flee a school of herring, but the herring pursue the shrimp into the jaws of the swordfish and thus they themselves are eaten. What herring are left after the swordfish has gorged on them are eaten by the gulls.

The open ocean holds hazards for Scomber as well. Fishermen with seine nets threaten his school. Carson had mentioned to Henrik van Loon that man must not come into the book "except from the fishes' viewpoint as a predator and destroyer," and indeed as operators of the trawl and seine nets they do seem to be just that; for one moment, however, Carson penetrates the imagination a curious fisherman who had often wondered, "What had the eyes of the mackerel seen? Things he'd never see; places he'd never go. . . . It seemed to him incongruous that a creature that had made a go of life in the sea, that had run the gauntlet of all the relentless enemies that he knew roved through that dimness his eyes could not penetrate, should at last come to death on the deck of a mackerel seiner, slimed with fish gurry and slippery with scales" (*USW*, 200). In the fisherman's momentary thought Carson puts forth the idea that human beings know far too little about the ocean. What, indeed, should their role be in relation to the sea?

Scomber is one of the mackerel who escapes the fishermen's nets and the raiding dogfish who gather at their edges to feed. As book 2 closes, Scomber, "traveling far below the surface," moves instinctively southwest. "He was going to a place he himself had never known – the deep, quiet waters along the edge of the continental shelf, off the Cape of Virginia" (*USW*, 206), where neither Carson nor her readers can follow.

Book 3: "River and Sea"

Book 3 follows Anguilla, the eel, from her home in the fictitious Bittern Pond to the sea, where she will mate. Anguilla, the largest eel in Bittern Pond, has lived there for 10 years. Twice in her life she makes the same 200-mile journey, once as an elver when she comes to the pond from the ocean where she was born to live on crayfish, water beetles, small frogs, and other pond creatures, and once as an adult when she makes the reverse journey to return.

Aware of the dearth of scientific knowledge of the eels' journey from their river homes to their spawning places in the deep ocean, Carson is, nonetheless, able to give a vivid picture of a representative journey through Anguilla (whose name is, once again, the species name for the common eel). The eels, Carson speculates, "followed the contours of the gently sloping continental shelf, descending the drowned valleys of their native rivers that had cut channels across the coastal plain in sunshine millions of years ago" (*USW*, 256). By whatever instinct they travel, Anguilla and her sister roe eels (only females make the journey back to their spawning grounds) make their way to the "deepest abyss of the Atlantic. There the young were to be born of the darkness of the deep sea and the old eels were to die and become sea again (*USW*, 256).

Once again in book 3 Carson reasserts her sense of the eternal cycles of the sea that give *Under the Sea Wind* an almost mythic dimension. In reference to the deep waters to which Anguilla is destined, Carson describes the eternal process of decay and regeneration. All creatures live for a space and then die, and when they do, "they are dissolved and made one with the sea" (*USW*, 262). In the depths of the abyss life is dissolved "to be used over and over again in the fashioning of other creatures" (*USW*, 263), so that the material immortality to which Carson referred is endlessly regenerated. There is no light, very little sound, and no human scrutiny of this part of the ocean depth. Rather, it is like a Jungian collective unconscious, the repository of the world soul.

There is in Carson's first book recognition of a world beyond human knowledge in which, in fact, we all participate. Thus, the correlation to the collective unconscious is apt. Frieda Fordham, in her *Introduction to Jung's Psychology*, states, "The conscious aspect of the psyche might be compared to an island rising from the sea – we only see the part above the water, but a much vaster unknown realm spreads below, and this could be likened to the unconscious."[5] That analogy is important in understanding the extent to which Carson's exploration of the sea may reflect her quest, both scientific and poetic, for an understanding of the natural world. Throughout *Under the Sea Wind* there is speculation about the mysteries that lie beneath the surface of the sea. Not only the fisherman puzzles over the nature of the life of the mackerel he sees dying on the deck of his ship; Carson herself ponders the mysteries that lie beyond the investigation of the scientist.

Under the Sea Wind is first an accurate scientific discussion of the cycles of birth and death, spring and fall, migration and return of the creatures of the sea. It is, moreover, a "series of descriptive narratives unfolding successively the life of the shore, the open sea, and the sea bottom" (foreword, *USW* 1941, xiv). It is also a recognition that, through these cycles, the life of the sea is as "nearly eternal as earthly life can be" (foreword, *USW* 1941, xiii). Finally, it is a recognition of the potent symbol that the sea is for the writer and for most human beings.

Publication

Had the publication date of *Under the Sea Wind* been more fortuitous, Carson's acclaim as a careful and literate nature writer might have come earlier. Since she still had her full-time job at the Bureau of Fisheries, the work proceeded slowly. Because of financial strains related to family and personal health problems, Carson often had to set aside the book and write brief articles for publication to make ends meet. Ultimately, she took three years to complete it, and its release in late 1941 met with favorable reviews. The *New York Times* said: "In this beautiful and unusual book a naturalist has reproduced a multitudinous 'picture of ocean life.' "[6] The *Baltimore Sun,* for whom Carson had written several nature pieces, said, "It is not alone that she deals simply and clearly with the curious and fascinating life of a mackerel, or an eel, or a skimmer. Miss Carson's language itself is of most extraordinary beauty, in its choice of words, in its imagery, in its restraint, and in its almost poetic cadence, so that at the close of a chapter it is difficult to say whether one is more pleased by the tale itself or by the manner of its telling."[7]

As mentioned in chapter 1 of this volume, the book was forgotten after the bombing of Pearl Harbor on 7 December 1941 brought America into World War II. It would be another 11 years before Carson would have another book about the sea to present to the public.

Conservation in Action

Shortly after the war, when she had returned to Washington from a brief stint in Chicago, she began to plan and conduct the research for the series Conservation in Action. Shirley Briggs, who worked with Carson on the first pamphlet in the series, *Chincoteague: A National Wildlife Refuge*, recalls that Carson was largely responsible for the conception, planning, and the execution of the series. "It was really her idea," said Briggs.[8] Certainly, Carson was responsible for the research and writing of five of the pamphlets produced between 1947 and 1950. Carson, Briggs maintains, also wanted to make the publications of the Fish and Wildlife Service more distinguished and professional in appearance than they had been in the past. Consequently, the series was produced on high-quality paper, with cleaner, more professional printing and a combination of skillful photography and illuminating maps. The general statement Carson wrote to introduce each pamphlet in the series, a plea for preservation of the natural world, remained in use by the Fish and Wildlife Service for more than 25 years.

Conservation, Carson had begun to feel, was central to the Fish and Wildlife Service's mandate, and Briggs wonders how many people who use the phrase "conservation in action" know who coined it.[9] In keeping with Carson's concerns for conservation, the pamphlet on the Chincoteague refuge in Virginia opens with a strong appeal for the preservation of migratory birds by creating protected areas in their flyways. Carson was at pains to point out that the Atlantic flyway, which Chincoteague serves, had experienced a sharp decline in the numbers of ducks and geese in the 1930s: "Once there were plenty of natural hostelries for the migrants. That was before our expanding civilization had drained the marshes, polluted the waters, substituted resort towns for wilderness. That was in the days when hunters were few."[10] Birds, Carson understood, needed food, rest, and security from hunters if their numbers were ever to begin to increase. Her agency wanted to reverse the decline of many of the migratory waterfowl on the Atlantic flyway, and Carson's pamphlet was as much an appeal for public support for that goal as it was an educational tool to help Americans understand the necessity of creating and maintaining the wildlife refuges.

Many of the birds who wintered or stopped in their migration at Chincoteague refuge were in desperate need of protection. Snow geese, whose numbers had been decimated in the 1930s, were unprotected in Canada. Thus, Carson reasoned, all the more need for Americans to do what they could to maintain the species. The same was true for migratory shore birds whose long annual migration took them from the northernmost limits of Greenland to the southernmost edges of South America. The vast tracts of agricultural development in South America had severely reduced their nesting areas, and many countries in their flyways had not restricted shooting; the wildlife refuges in the United States, from Moosehorn, Maine, to Savannah, Georgia, were the hope for their survival.

Carson and Briggs visited Chincoteague together, and as seriously as they took their work, Briggs recalls the enjoyment they got from it. Briggs recounts one story that reveals the sense of humor Carson's friends remember. Briggs, a photographer and illustrator, often had to use a black changing bag to load film into her camera. Carson thought the process so peculiar that she would make Briggs load and unload her camera in the strange black bag in the middle of the hotel lobby. Briggs has captured the escapade in an illustration she did for Carson (Briggs, 9 July 1991).

There were times, of course, when the business of researching the pamphlets was quite serious. The second pamphlet, *Parker River: A National Wildlife Refuge,* required Carson and her photographer/illustrator, Katherine L. Howe, to go to the river's coastal marshes in Essex County, Massachusetts. Area residents were very unhappy with the idea of having a refuge in their county, and correspondence between Katherine Howe and Shirley Briggs indicates that Howe thought that the color film taken at the refuge was deliberately sabotaged by a man who offered to get it developed for her.[11]

The Parker River Refuge was, according to Carson, "New England's most important contribution to the national effort to save the waterfowl of North America,"[12] Carson saw this refuge as a companion sanctuary to Chincoteague, as it was on the same Atlantic flyway. Many of the same species that rested and fed at Parker River traveled on to Chincoteague either to winter or to rest before journeying further south.

That refuges are important to the maintenance and increase of migratory bird populations was abundantly clear at Parker River. "In the spring of 1944, about 2,000 waterfowl used the refuge. Two years later, the spring count was nearly 15,000" (*Parker River*, 1). Carson's study focuses on why it was so important to maintain a sanctuary at this particular point in the flyway. Since waterfowl have flyways that almost never change from generation to generation, it was necessary for the Fish and Wildlife Service to find areas within the flyways that offered the necessary food for the birds. Plum Island, the center of the Parker River Refuge, offered ocean beach, dunes, thickets, salt meadows, and tidal flats; thus, it was the obvious choice for a stopover on the long migratory route of the many species who rested there.

To convince the skeptic of the choice location and environment of Parker River, she asks the reader to take a bird's-eye view and imagine what it is like to see Parker River Refuge from the top of an army observation tower located on the dunes. Here one sees all the variety of the sanctuary and understands its relationship to the whole series of refuges on the flyway.

Carson is not, however, indifferent to the problems of the human inhabitants and is careful to emphasize that the Fish and Wildlife Service is well aware of the importance of the soft-shelled clam industry to area residents. This ability to see the larger picture and to show the unhappy residents how the refuge and the clam industry can live in harmony again illustrates Carson's focus on the necessity for all species to live in harmony. While *Under the Sea Wind* shows human beings as predators and destroyers, the Parker

River pamphlet shows how careful regulation allows bird habitat and human industry to coexist. Helping people to see their place in the environment and showing them how to live in harmony with the world around them increasingly became the focus of Carson's writing.

If the Parker River is essential to the northern part of the Atlantic flyway, Mattamuskeet Wildlife Refuge and two other refuges in North Carolina "provide winter food and shelter for more than 100,000 waterfowl."[13] During Carson's time at the service, Mattamuskeet was one of the few southern refuges in the flyway and one of the last resting places for the birds before they left the United States and entered the hostile territory in the West Indies and South America. Only two others – one in South Carolina and one in Georgia – then existed. While today there are more refuges in Florida and Texas, birds remain unprotected outside North America.

In *Mattamuskeet: A National Wildlife Refuge,* Carson deals directly with the question of why the Fish and Wildlife Service has established and managed the refuges along the Atlantic flyway. She asks what many of her readers perhaps would like to ask: "What does the Mattamuskeet refuge do for the waterfowl that could not be done in the same area of wild country without management?" (*Mattamuskeet,* 6). In the answer that Carson gives is an indication of her own thinking on conservation. Aside from making the refuge "many times more productive of natural food" than unmanaged areas, management is there to let nature take its course. "Underlying and determining the character of the management activities," she writes, "are the great recurrent rhythms of nature. Moving over the marshlands, as over a stage, the passing seasons bring the cyclic sweep of two great series of events, one in the animal world, the other in the world of plants. The two cycles, are directly related" (*Mattamuskeet,* 7). The recurrent rhythms and the cycles of nature are what Carson sees as the motivator and the controller of the refuge. The Fish and Wildlife Service is there to protect those cycles from outside interference and to regulate the production of food, so that the migrating birds will always be sufficiently fed. Nature has found the perfect cycles, and human beings must find a way to fit themselves into those recurring cycles without destroying them.

In 1950 Carson wrote *Bear River: A National Wildlife Refuge.* She ventured beyond the Atlantic flyway to describe a refuge in Utah, on the border between the Central and Pacific flyways. Here the problems were slightly different for the service because "water and conflict for water use dominate the history of the area."[14] Carson again set out to show her readers how important the balance between human needs and wildlife needs is to the conservation of a variety of species. As in the other pamphlets, conservation, management, and restricted use are the keys. The Fish and Wildlife Service at Bear River must balance the conflict between civilization and the wilderness, Carson believed, for the refuge is important not simply locally. "The millions of feathered visitors that congregate there during migration will spread out widely over the continent" (*Bear River*, 11).

Another Conservation in Action pamphlet that Carson wrote, *Guarding Our Wildlife Resources*, broadened the scope of the other pamphlets.[15] Here Carson discusses migratory birds, big game animals, endangered species, marine fisheries, and national and international cooperation in conservation efforts. In effect it is an overview of America's wildlife resources and of the need for international cooperation to protect wildlife for generations to come.

Conclusion

What marks Carson's early writing about the sea and her work for the Fish and Wildlife Service is her growing awareness of the integral connection of all aspects of the environment and of the need for some agency to protect wildlife from the rapacious hand of industry. Related to this is the sense that the natural world is far larger and more complex than human beings have yet discovered, and the destruction of one element in the finely balanced web will, indeed, have an impact on all other elements. Thus while nature prunes species harshly, there is a natural ebb and flow of species dominance (as illustrated in the death of the owls in *Under the Sea Wind*). When human beings destroy species, as the white settlers did around the Bear River refuge and as hunters did along the Atlantic flyway, nature cannot so easily repair the damage. This emphasis on conservation and on the mysterious interconnection of all life becomes the hallmark of Carson's later books about the sea and is central to *Silent Spring*.

Chapter Three

Fame

The Sea around Us

If Carson's life changed radically when she decided in college to major in biology instead of literature, a second radical change occurred with the 1951 publication of *The Sea around Us*. Rachel Carson became famous. While her first book had been overwhelmed by historical events and was silently consigned to remainders, her second book had quite a different publication history. Perhaps the biggest thing that happened to give Carson's name recognition was that William Shawn, editor of the *New Yorker*, decided to profile several chapters. Usually, the *New Yorker* "Profile" focused on the life and work of a famous individual, but he was so taken with Carson's book that he offered her what amounted to more than a year's salary at her government job for excerpts from *The Sea around Us* (Brooks, 123). But even before the *New Yorker* serial, which ran on 2, 9, and 16 June 1951, the *Yale Review* had published the chapter "The Birth of an Island" in September 1950; this won Carson the $1,000 George Westinghouse Science Writing Award.

Despite this flurry of interest in the book just prior to its publication, the process of writing it had not been an easy one. Still a full-time government employee at the Fish and Wildlife Service, Carson wrote *The Sea around Us*, as she had *Under the Sea Wind*, while competing responsibilities vied for her time and attention. She knew she wanted to write more about the sea even though her first publisher, Simon and Schuster, was not willing to commit to a contract for a second book. She wrote to William Beebe in 1948 that "the book I am writing is something I have had in mind for a good while. I have had to wait to undertake it until at least a part of the wartime oceanic studies should be published" (Brooks, 110).

The fact that Carson worked for the government and had, during the war, been involved in much of the discussion about tide tables, troop movements, and other vital wartime information about the sea gave her access to up-to-date findings and much new oceanographic information. In that respect, Carson's government job was a benefit to her writing, but in almost no other respect was her employment a boon. When she received the Eugene F. Saxton Memorial Fellowship in 1949 and took unpaid time off to work on the book, she had to work more than twice as hard when she returned to the office, so that she could not give any attention to the book at all. Given these constraints, the final publication date had to be revised.

While writing the book, she also took time, at William Beebe's suggestion, to go to Florida and get her "head under water" (Sterling, 118) During this same period, she also went aboard the *Albatross III* to study the contours of the ocean floor. She later wrote in an unpublished, undated piece, "Origins of the Book, *The Sea around Us*," probably composed several months after the publication of *The Sea around Us,* that "the high point of the cruise was 'seeing,' with the aid of the echo-sounder, the great undersea canyons that cut into the outer rim of Georges Bank. It was an extremely dramatic thing to watch the level ocean floor pass beneath us, then suddenly drop away in a deep, V-shaped chasm" (Beinecke papers).

With the war, Carson's own demanding work, and family responsibilities, the book was literally a decade in the making. The actual writing probably took a little more than three years, but Carson herself said in "Origins" that it was a book that she had been working on all her life; since she was a child she had read everything she could about the ocean. Her work at Woods Hole, Massachusetts, where she spent several summers, added a new dimension to her study. The sea filled Carson with questions, and she used the facilities at Woods Hole to try to find some answers. In fact, Carson continues in "Origins," "the genesis of *The Sea around Us* belongs to that first year at Woods Hole, when I began storing away facts about the sea."

For the structure of her second book Carson turned once again to "Undersea." She wanted to enlarge what she had done in her first book, and the tightly constructed *Atlantic* essay was a good starting point. Carson wanted to avoid writing "another introduction to oceanography" (Brooks, 124). While her research was meticulous as ever ("the backbone of the work for *The Sea around Us* . . . was just plain hard slogging – searching in the often dry and exceedingly technical papers of scientists for the kernels of fact to weld into my profile of the sea," she writes in "Origins"), her ultimate goal was to portray the life of the sea in words nontechnical readers would understand. Carson was, perhaps, writing the book she would have liked to have read as a young woman to satisfy her own hunger to know about the oceans.

Into the Sea

Water is life, so Carson went back to the beginning of time to start *The Sea around Us.* She also emphasized the sea as source by calling the first part of the book, which is about the beginnings and the growth of the oceans, "Mother Sea." Here again is the cyclic pattern that was so successful in *Under the Sea Wind*, and the reader sees the process by which constant rain made the sea. Time – centuries, millions of years – passes before the reader's eyes as "worms evolved, and starfish, and hard-shelled creatures with many-jointed legs, the anthropods."[1] Mountains rise and fall, are worn away while the sea continues its relentless work, yet scientists have only the "past 500 million years . . . preserved [in] the fossil record" (*SAU*, 9). The sense of immensity, and the infinitely patient process creating water, life, land, and creatures is captured in Carson's opening chapter, "The Grey Beginnings."

We all have our beginnings in this process, and Carson points to the scientific validation of our link with mother sea: "Each of us carries in our veins a salty stream in which the elements sodium, potassium, and calcium are combined in almost the same proportions as in sea water. This is our inheritance from the day, untold millions of years ago, when a remote ancestor, having progressed from the one-cellular to the many-cellular stage, first developed a circulatory system in which the fluid was merely the water of the sea" (*SAU*, 13).

Carson reasserts the connections between all life and the sea. It is truly mother sea: "And as life itself began in the sea, so each of us begins his individual life in a miniature ocean with his mother's womb, and in the stages of his embryonic development repeats the steps by which his race evolved, from gill-breathing inhabitants of a water world to creatures able to live on land" (*SAU*, 14).

Linked to our primal connection with the sea is our continued fascination with it. Carson's childhood longing for the ocean convinced her that we all share in our bones (our skeletons are a "heritage from the calcium-rich ocean of Cambrian time" [*SAU*, 13]) and in our blood the longing to return to the sea.

Human beings did return to the sea, but only on the sea's terms, and this for Carson confirms the centrality of the ocean in the life of the earth and its creatures. Of human return to the ocean, Carson points out: "And yet he has returned to his mother sea only on her own terms. He cannot control or change the ocean as, in his brief tenancy of earth, he has subdued and plundered the continents. In the artificial world of his cities and towns, he often forgets the true nature of his planet. . . . And then, as never on land, he knows the truth that his world is a water world, a planet dominated by its covering mantle of ocean, in which the continents are but transient intrusions of land above the surface of the all-encircling sea" (*SAU*, 15). Carson made her first trip underwater in researching the book, around the coral reefs of southern Florida, and it undoubtedly influenced her imaginative experience of the sea. Her epigram for chapter 2, a quote from Herman Melville's *Moby-Dick*, reaffirms that Carson's interest in the oceans has a greater dimension than the purely technical or "scientific":

> There is, one knows not what sweet mystery about this sea, whose gently awful stirrings seem to speak of some hidden soul beneath.

One of the most intriguing phenomena described by Carson is the drifting weeds of the Sargasso Sea. While Carson relates the controversy among scientists about the origin of the weeds (whether they are blown out from coastal beds or are self-perpetuating), she is less interested in taking sides than she is in the phenomenon of the weeds themselves. Carson suggests, "It might well be that some of the very weeds you would see if you visited the place today were seen by Columbus and his men" (*SAU*, 27). Some plants do die, but others replace them. There is in the weeds a metaphor to which Carson always returns – the endless cycles in the sea, each contributing to others in a sort of "material immortality." Understanding how that material immortality endures is her goal. "Once, when her mother told her that God created the world, Rachel replied, 'Yes, and General Motors created my Oldsmobile. But how is the question.' "[2]

The process of the material immortality of the weeds is central to Carson's question about the sea. How did the sea come to be; how did the land rise from it; how, given that process, does humanity fit in? These are the questions that pervade *The Sea around Us*. Carson's fundamental answer is that the sea determines everything. If Carson was unimpressed with the fact that God made the world, she was certainly impressed with the ingenuity with which the sea endured; her tone throughout *The Sea around Us* implies a reverence for the ocean that borders on the religious.

Adding to the mystery of the ocean for Carson is the fact that about half of the planet "is covered by miles-deep, lightless water, that has been dark since the world began" (*SAU*, 37). When Carson first began her work on the book, only two men, William Beebe and Otis Barton, had ever gone beyond the range of "visible light." The mystery of that dark half of the world drew Carson in, and one of her goals was "to reconstruct in imagination these eerie, forbidding regions" (*SAU*, 39).

Human Influence and Insignificance

One of the outstanding differences between Carson's second book and her first is the role that human beings play. In *Under the Sea Wind* fishermen intruded on the lives of the fish and the shore-dwelling birds. In fact, it was the human element that seemed always to upset the delicate balance of nature. In the second book, Carson is fascinated by the processes scientists have used to understand the ocean.

Carson points out that prior to World War II naval oceanographers knew precious little about the sea. She quotes one naval officer as saying the United States learned a "most frightening lesson" about the "almost desperate lack of basic information on the fundamentals of the nature of the sea" (*SAU*, 113). This vacuum prompted military concern, since victory depended heavily on the transfer of troops and supplies across water. During the war the United States considerably escalated its research on the seas. One result of this, which Carson mentions in the 1961 revised edition of the book, was a system to warn the Pacific Islands of the coming of seismic sea waves caused by undersea earthquakes. For example, in 1960, when earthquakes on the coast of Chile created seismic waves, "reporters from the scattered tide stations gave ample notice that a seismic wave had formed and was spreading across the Pacific" (*SAU*, 127). The result of the warnings was that, while there was property damage on the Hawaiian Islands, there was very little loss of life. Japan, which disregarded the U.S. warning about the wave, was not nearly so fortunate. Information on tides, undersea mountain ranges, and ocean depths was scanty before World War II, so Carson had a wealth of new material to work with in the writing of her second book.

This new research, as Carson acknowledges, also changed the nature of scientific work on the sea. Scientists were able to conduct much more sophisticated field work on ocean sediments which, in turn, revealed much about the earth itself. For example, in the chapter "The Long Snowfall," Carson describes how scientists took samples of the ocean sediments to uncover the history of the earth. This chapter illustrates once again how Carson can integrate scientific information with an almost poetic message about the sea. She writes: "The sediments are a sort of epic poem of the earth. When we are wise enough, perhaps we can read in them all of past history. For all is written here. . . . The dramatic and the catastrophic in earth history have left their trace in the sediments – the outpourings of volcanoes, the advance and retreat of the ice, the searing aridity of desert lands, the sweeping destruction of floods" (*SAU*, 27).

In the work of scientists, Carson sees a harmonious relationship between human beings and their environment. Nature holds secrets that scientists are slowly demystifying. As Carson saw it, the ideal stance of scientists in relation to the world, and especially to the sea, is that of seekers of truth. The object is not to conquer the oceans or to change the relentless patterns of the restless sea but to understand them better. It is when the intent is mercenary or conquistadorial that nature is threatened, and human beings ultimately lose.

"The Birth of an Island" is the chapter that best exemplifies Carson's attitude toward those who would despoil nature. In it Carson's tone changes noticeably. First she describes in detail the process of birth. The millions of years involved in the building of an island is encapsulated in the opening paragraph, where Carson recapitulates how Bermuda came to sit in the Atlantic Ocean. The creation of an island, she points out, is "violent, explosive, earth-shaking. . . . It is one of the paradoxes in the ways of earth and sea that a process seemingly so destructive, so catastrophic in nature, can result in an act of creation" (*SAU*, 84). Set against that paradox is another. It is hard to imagine that the seemingly harmless process of landing a few goats on an island can lead to so much destruction, but it does. The explorers of the South Pacific Islands had no idea of the consequences of their behavior, but the results were earth shattering.

Before those disastrous consequences are revealed, however, Carson, species by species, populates her island. "No less than the water, the winds and the air currents play their part in bringing inhabitants to the islands. The upper atmosphere, even during the ages before man entered it in his machines, was a place of congested traffic" (*SAU*, 90). Spiders, aerial plankton, living insects, all are wafted by currents to the newly formed island. Birds also bring their share of flora and fauna: "Charles Darwin raised eighty-two separate plants, belonging to five distinct species" from a mud ball extracted from a bird's feathers (*SAU*, 91). In the processes of nature, islands also die. An example of that is Krakatoa, which exploded in a volcanic eruption in 1883. Certainly it was the most cataclysmic death the modern world has witnessed, but Carson points out that islands rise and sink with a fair degree of regularity.

Islands are by their very nature unstable, but while they live in the ocean, nature populates them with a bright array of unusual species. Because there is very little opportunity for cross-breeding, marvellous species of extraordinary tameness and vulnerability have developed. And herein lies humanity's tragic blunder. Unlike Carson's scientist, the explorer is not interested in preserving and studying the fragile balance of nature that exists on these most delicate outcroppings in the sea. Rather, he is interested in using the islands for his own ends. "Man, unhappily, has written one of his blackest records as a destroyer on the oceanic islands. He has seldom set foot on an island that he has not brought about disastrous changes. He has destroyed environments by cutting, clearing, and burning; he has brought with him as a chance associate the nefarious rat; and almost invariably he has turned loose upon the island a whole Noah's Ark of goats, hogs, cattle, dogs, cats, and other non-native animals as well as plants. Upon species after species of island life, the black night of extinction has fallen" (*SAU*, 93).

A shipwreck can spell extinction for species of island birds who have no defenses against the rats that swim ashore. Carson quotes Ernst Mayr, who wrote in 1918 of the extinction of the birds of Lord

Howe Island: "This paradise of birds has become a wilderness, and the quietness of death reigns where all was melody" (*SAU*, 94).

In "The Birth of an Island" Carson's conservationist instincts, which were so much a part of the Conservation in Action series, reassert themselves. In the earlier chapters she was scientist recounting the history of the sea's birth and growth. Here her tone changes from poetic to polemic: "Most of man's habitual tampering with nature's balance by introducing exotic species has been done in ignorance of the fatal chain of events that would follow. But in modern times, at least, we might profit by history" (*SAU*, 95). The litany of man's destruction follows: Trinidad, Laysan, the Hawaiian Islands, Lord Howe Island, Tristan da Cunha – all experienced the scourge of human exploration. Unfortunately, thinks Carson, people do not learn from history. They tend to repeat it and thus unthinkingly create the ultimate disaster – extinction. "The tragedy of the oceanic islands lies in the uniqueness, the irreplaceability of the species they have developed by the slow processes of the ages. In a reasonable world men would have treated these islands as precious possessions, as natural museums filled with beautiful and curious works of creation, valuable beyond price because nowhere in the world are they duplicated" (*SAU*, 96).

The force of the sea and the eternal pull it has on the land closes the first section of the *The Sea around Us* and begins the second. Carson reports that the seas are rising, and all along the coasts of America there is "a steady, but continuing advance of the sea upon the land" (*SAU*, 98). Carson points out that the process is a natural one. The sea is reclaiming the land as it has done periodically over the millennia. "What is happening is nothing new. Over the long span of geologic time, the ocean waters have come in over North America many times and have again retreated into their basins. For the boundary between sea and land is the most fleeting and transitory feature of the earth, and the sea is forever repeating its encroachments upon the continents" (*SAU*, 97). Here again, Carson returns to the cyclic metaphors she used so poetically in her first book. It is the constant ebb and flow of the tide, the rising and falling of the sea, that is a constant in the life of the earth. It is not human activity that endures, but natural cycles.

Human insignificance in the face of nature's force is illustrated in Carson's chapter on wind and water. Human beings have no defense against the fury of the sea when it strikes the land, and they can do little more than measure the power; they cannot leash it. From the Pacific Coast to the Shetland and Orkney Islands the sea creates "perverse and freakish doings" (*SAU*, 121), and human beings can keep a record of their own insignificance. It is in the middle section of the book that the sea's power and its uncontrollable energy is catalogued as it wears away at the land. Britain, an island that has always been conscious of the "powerful marine gnawing," has lists of towns "washed away by the sea," or "lost by the sea" (*SAU*, 123).

But what seems like chaos and destruction to those on the shore is a part of an interplay of earth, air, and water, and nowhere is this more evident to Carson than in the great currents of the Atlantic and Pacific Oceans. Human ignorance of these currents is recounted in a story of English packet ships. Americans wanted to know why it took two weeks longer for British mail packets to reach America than it did for American packets to reach England. Benjamin Franklin investigated the problem and found that American sailors used the Gulf Stream to their advantage, whereas British sea captains ignored its existence. American whalers had found that whales stayed out of the stream, and they did too, but British ships actually tried to sail within it and were confronted by a current of almost three miles an hour. The British ignored Franklin's information and continued to sail against the current.

Finally, the enduring power of the restless sea is illustrated in the story of the Convoluta, a worm with, as Carson says, "no distinction of appearance" (*SAU*, 162). The worm, however, is distinct in its behavior; it rises out of the sand when the tide ebbs and literally sits in the sun. When the tide flows in the worm sinks back into the sand. The story of the instinctive behavior of the little worm would not seem unusual except for the fact that when scientists take them into laboratories and put them in aquaria without tides, the worms exhibit the same behavior: "Twice each day Convoluta rises out of the sand on the bottom of the aquarium, into the light of the sun. And twice each day it sinks again into the sand. Without a brain, or what we would call a memory, or even any very clear perception, Convoluta continues to live out its life in this alien place, remembering, in every fiber of its small green body, the tidal rhythm of the distant sea" (*SAU*, 162-63).

If T. S. Eliot could say of the Mississippi, "I don't know much about God, but I think that the river is a strange brown God," Carson also seems to be saying that the powers of the sea are so mysterious as to seem godlike. While her colleague Shirley Briggs asserts that Carson was not a mystic (Briggs, 9 July 1991), there is in her reverence for the enduring rhythms of the sea a recognition that it is beyond human control or maybe even understanding.

The Sea and Climate

In the final section of *The Sea around Us*, "Man and the Sea about Him," Carson once again returns to the themes of her first article. The sea is the womb of life; it is generator and grave for all. It is the alpha and omega of the planet. Given that, she articulates human curiosity about the sea and about how the sea and the land are interconnected and how human life is also controlled by the forces of the sea. Literature can recount but cannot control the life of the sea, but the sea controls the life of the land and consequently human life. Most impressive of the sea's effects on the land is its effect on climate. Using the research of Otto Pettersson, who studied the currents around his native Sweden, Carson explains how changes in global climate result from changes in ocean currents.

The history of European climatic changes can be studied in light of the changes in the currents of the Atlantic. The cycles of underwater tides are also important to Europe, and Pettersson's study of them revealed why the herring left Swedish waters and began to populate the waters around the Netherlands. The changes in the deep waves of the Gulmarfiord heralded "the changing fortunes of the Swedish herring fishery" (*SAU*, 175). But Sweden's loss was Holland's gain, and someday the deep waves may return to Sweden, and Holland will feel the loss.

Currents and submarine waves have, like the rest of the ocean's movement, patterns that can be tracked if not controlled. Through careful astronomical studies, Pettersson discovered that the underwater tides were "at their greatest strength during the closing centuries of the Middle Ages. . . . Only about every eighteen centuries do the heavenly bodies assume this particular relation" (*SAU*, 176) that causes the giant tides. Carson then went to Scandinavian folklore to see what relation these tides had to the lives of the people. She found evidence that the earth had once been warmer and could indeed be warming again under the influence of changes in the Gulf Stream and the underground waves. The sea brought abundance to Sweden for a time and then gave it to Holland. The sea also gave abundance to Greenland for a time, then took it back, and the early Scandinavian in lore preserves a record of that abundance.

Pettersson, Carson tells her readers, developed "a theory of climatic variation . . . He showed that there are alternating periods of mild and severe climates that correspond to the long-period cycles of oceanic tides. The world's most recent period of maximum tides, and most rigorous climate, occurred about 1433, its effect being felt, however, for several centuries before and after that year. The minimum tidal effect prevailed about A.D. 550, and it will occur again about the year 2400" (*SAU*, 177). Pettersson's theory is corroborated by early lore that depicts "the abundant fruit of excellent quality growing in Greenland, and of the number of cattle that could be pastured there" (*SAU*, 177).

The Scandinavian colonists of Iceland and Greenland witnessed a cooling of the Atlantic waters that killed the fruit of Greenland, brought the Eskimos further south to make raids for food on the Norwegian settlers, and finally destroyed the colonies. By the early fourteenth century "packs of wolves crossed on the ice from Norway to Denmark. The entire Baltic froze over, forming a bridge of solid ice between Sweden and the Danish Islands" (*SAU*, 178). The fourteenth century witnessed a number of catastrophic weather phenomena that marked the coldest part of the cycles of tides. After that there was a gradual warming which Pettersson speculated may well continue for hundreds more years.

Carson was not simply interested in the way currents and undersea waves affect climates; she was also concerned, in a manner that looks forward to *Silent Spring*, with what human beings did with that knowledge. She recognized in the early 1950s a persistent idea: deliberately changing "the pattern of the current and so modifying climate at will" (*SAU*, 167). She even points out that sometime around 1912 Congress was asked for money to construct a jetty that would cause the Gulf Stream to "swing nearer the mainland of the northern United States" (*SAU*, 168). This, it was reasoned, would bring warmer winters to the northern part of the United States. Even if such a project were feasible, Carson writes, the results would have been contrary to expectations: the weather along the Atlantic coast of North America would have become far worse. Carson observes about the sea: "For the globe as a whole, the ocean is the great regulator, the great stabilizer of temperatures" (*SAU*, 170). When human beings try to control the sea instead of living within its immutable laws, they unwittingly do the greatest damage to themselves.

Poetry in Science

Human beings have yet to fathom all the mysteries of the ocean. As late as 1989, Jeffrey S. Levington, in his afterword to a new edition of *The Sea around Us*, pointed out that "those who never leave the edge of the sea may know little less than those who have voyaged across, or the diver who has touched the ocean floor" (*SAU*, 213). More than 30 years after Carson's revised edition of *The Sea around Us* appeared, we are confronted with the ocean's boundless mystery and its endless power over both our lives and our imaginations. "For all at last return to the sea – to Oceanus, the ocean river, like the ever-flowing stream of time, the beginning and the end" (*SAU*, 212).

Thor Heyerdal, who corresponded with Carson on research for *The Sea around Us*, wrote to her on 18 May 1951 after reading the book: "It does good to see that a serious and conscientious writer can grasp the fascinating sides of the science and the beauty of the sea and its story in such a way as you have mastered it" (Beinecke papers). Clearly the approach that Carson took, writing a series of beautiful word portraits of the sea in different settings and poses, integrated with a meticulous scientific accuracy, important scientific information, and a poetic sense of the sea gave her book a rare harmoniousness. She even left out material that she felt would upset the overall tenor of the book.

"The Ocean and a Hungry World" was deleted from the book just before publication on Carson's instructions. Her own typescript indicates that this was to be the last chapter in the book. Her note, dated November 1963, indicates that it was omitted "on my own decision" (Beinecke papers). The chapter has a different tone from the previous ones, in which the sea's voice dominates. Here Carson sounds more the agent of the Fish and Wildlife Service than the curious scientist or reverent witness. She catalogs the way people fish and discusses attempts to broaden the catch to increase the yield for food. She even looks into the possibilities of fish farming. She recognizes a problem – feeding millions – and she speculates about possible resources for solving the problem. What the chapter lacks – and what Carson must have seen that it lacks – is the lyricism so in evidence in the rest of the book. It is utilitarian, and Carson rejected it despite the value of the research.

Life after *The Sea around Us*

The intense prepublication interest in *The Sea around Us* was matched by postpublication reviews. Carson was widely praised, and most reviewers saw in the book the exquisite blend of science and poetry that she had achieved. The book was a Book-of-the-Month-Club alternative selection, it was abridged by *Reader's Digest,* and it won both the John Burroughs Medal and the National Book Award (Brooks, 127). For the first time in her life, Carson was without financial worries. She could begin her next book free of many of the constraints forced upon her by her job with the Fish and Wildlife Service.

During the 10 years between the release of the first edition in 1951 and of the revised edition in 1961 much happened in Carson's life. She finished, in record time, *The Edge of the Sea* (1955) to nearly the same critical acclaim that was accorded *The Sea around Us*. She also wrote the magazine article, "Help Your Child to Wonder," which she planned to turn into a full-length children's book. And she had a protracted correspondence with Ruth Nanda Anshen, general editor of Harper and Brothers' World Perspective Series, about writing a book for the series, tentatively titled "The Origins of Life."

Carson's correspondence with Anshen continued through 5 June 1963, when Carson wrote to her, "In October I am giving a lecture at the Kaiser Foundation in San Francisco as a contribution to a symposium on 'Man and His Environment.' Another lecture on essentially this same theme is scheduled for the Mayo Clinic's Centennial Celebration in the fall of 1964. I have recently been invited to give one of the Leon Lectures at the University of Pennsylvania sometime next year on a date to be determined. My reason for telling you all this is that it is my present plan to shape these lectures in such a way that they will form the framework of your volume. In this way I shall be able to accomplish two separate purposes at the same time" (Beinecke papers).

With all her plans, Carson, during this 10-year correspondence with Anshen, never did focus her attention fully on the book. She had already contracted with Houghton Mifflin to do *The Edge of the Sea*, she had undertaken a revision of *The Sea around Us*, and she was committed to the work on the young readers' edition being abridged and edited by Anne Terry White. She was, from 1958 until the time of her death, deeply involved with researching, writing, and defending *Silent Spring*. She had even begun to realize that the World Perspectives topic no longer suited her primary interest, the exploitation and pollution of the environment. As early as 27 February 1957, Marie Rodell wrote to Anshen on Carson's behalf: "Rachel feels that, in view of Julian Huxley's book, *Evolution in Action*, the emphasis in her proposed book should be shifted. She feels that the relation of life to its environment is at the core of her original idea of the book and lends itself to fresher material and material less like Mr. Huxley's than the emphasis on evolution itself" (Beinecke Papers).

The correspondence continued, with Anshen offering encouragement and Carson continuing to express interest, but in rather vague terms. On 8 April 1961 Anshen wrote: "I hope that you will allow me to express my abiding eagerness to learn from you that your volume for World Perspectives will be completed in the visible future. Your honored place in the Series awaits your presence" (Beinecke Papers). Carson responded on 24 April: "I do look forward to a day when we can talk about our book. In spite of the lack of visible progress, it continues to grow in my mind, and I feel it may be the most important of my books" (Beinecke papers).

While Carson never did work on the book for the World Perspectives Series, the time between the publication of *The Sea around Us* and her death was an incredibly fruitful period, reflecting the sharpening focus her life was taking. By 1961, when she was finishing *Silent Spring*, she was also working on a preface to the revised edition of *The Sea around Us* that emphasized her concern that the sea was not safe from human intrusion. She wrote: "Although man's record as a steward of the natural resources of the earth has been a discouraging one, there has long been a certain comfort in the belief that the sea, at least, was inviolate, beyond his ability to change and to despoil. But this belief, unfortunately, has proved to be naive. In unlocking the secrets of the atom modern man has found himself confronted with a frightening problem – what to do with the most dangerous materials that have ever existed in all the Earth's history, the by-products of atomic fission. The stark dilemma that faces him is whether he can dispose of these lethal substances without rendering the earth uninhabitable" (*SAU*, xi).

Carson's fear, heightened by her research for *Silent Spring*, was that we might have gone beyond the point of no return in our abuse of atomic energy and toxic pesticides. This fear permeates the preface to the revised edition of *The Sea around Us*. She continued in the same ominous vein: "It is a curious situation that the sea, from which life first arose, should now be threatened by the activities of one form of that life. But the sea, though changed in a sinister way, will continue to exist; the threat is rather to life itself" (*SAU*, xiii).

The Edge of the Sea

The Edge of the Sea is a book very different from *The Sea around Us*. Carson began it under the most auspicious circumstances. She was without financial worries; she had a very good publisher and a sympathetic and interested editor, and she was no longer working for the Fish and Wildlife Service. She could devote all her time to travel and research. This period, from 1952 to 1958, might well have been the happiest of her life.

Immersion

Carson conceived of her third book as a sort of field guide to the flora and fauna of the shore. In it, she says, "I am telling something of the story of how that marvelous, tough, vital, and adaptable something we know as LIFE has come to occupy one part of the sea world and how it has adjusted itself and survived despite the immense, blind forces acting upon it from every side."[3]

As she grew older Carson was drawn more and more to the life of the sea. *The Edge of the Sea* is the book that allowed her the most freedom and leeway in what she studied and wrote about. She says in the preface, "To understand the shore, it is not enough to catalog its life. Understanding comes only when, standing on a beach, we can sense the long rhythms of earth and sea that sculptured its land forms and produced the rock and sand of which it is composed;

when we can sense with the eye and ear of the mind the surge of life beating always at its shore – blindly, inexorably pressing for a foothold."[4]

In researching the book Carson actually spent hours in tide pools with her illustrator, Bob Hines, collecting and examining specimens. Hines recounts a story of Carson's total immersion in her study: "Maine coastal waters are never warm, and the tide pools were often frigid, yet Rachel never hesitated to enter. Clad only in lightweight clothing and tennis shoes, she waded into the hip-deep water and became so engrossed in her research that she paid no attention to the time or how chilled she became. One cloudy day even her determination failed, and when she started to climb out of a pool, she was so numb she nearly fell back in. I splashed in beside her, picked her up, and carried her to the car" (Hines, 65).

Even in this narrowest of her books, Carson gives the reader a sense of the largeness of the sea and its connection with the land. As Carol Gartner points out, there is even a stylistic interconnection: "Interlocking paragraphs reflect environmental relationships. A description of periwinkles so persistently scraping rocks that they must constantly bring forward new teeth is followed by a discussion of the effects of the scraping on the rocks themselves."[5]

Carson points out early in the book that "the shore has a dual nature, changing with the swing of the tides, belonging now to the land, now to the sea. On the ebb tide it knows the harsh extremes of the land world, being exposed to heat and cold, to wind, to rain and drying sun. On the flood tide it is a water world, returning briefly to the relative stability of the open sea" (ES, 1).

Carson also explores the shore at night, making for one of the more romantic passages in the book:

> The blackness of the night possessed water, air, and beach. It was the darkness of an older world, before Man. . . . There was no other visible life – just one small crab near the sea . . . I was filled with the odd sensation that for the first time I knew the creature in its own world – that I understood, as never before, the essence of its being. In that moment time was suspended; the world to which I belonged did not exist and I might have been an onlooker from outer space. The little crab alone with the sea became a symbol that stood for life itself – for the delicate, destructible, yet incredibly vital force that somehow holds its place amid the harsh realities of the inorganic world."
> (ES, 5)

Interconnection and Adaptability

Grounding Carson's poetic immersion in her subject is the physical basis of her study: three coastlines. These are the rocky shores off the coast of Maine, the sandy shores of the middle and southern Atlantic states, and the coral reefs off the coast of southern Florida. These three types of shore do not simply represent three discrete studies of the life on the margins of the sea in the three locations; rather, they represent for Carson an orchestrated movement from North to South, from young to old, and from rigorous to more benign.

In her preliminary notes for the book, Carson wrote, "We are dealing with elemental problems – the relation of the living creature to his world; and with the cosmic phenomena by which vast and mysterious forces of the universe come into direct relation with even the smallest, the most fragile being" (Beinecke Papers). Her preliminary notes also indicate that Carson was looking for examples of interrelations to physics, geology, biochemistry, and ecology. She understood that she could not study any animal as an isolated species; hence she could not simply do a shore guide pointing out the different animals and plants. She saw that the life of the shore constituted a mysterious series of interconnections, which she would try to reveal through her book. Carson starred one of her own notes, which clearly focuses her concern:

> So even in the vast and mysterious reaches of the sea, we are brought back to the fundamental truth that nothing lives to itself. The water of the sea is changed, in its chemical nature and in its capacity for inducing metabolic change, by the fact that certain organisms have lived within it, by the fact that they have transmitted to the water a property it would have lacked had it not been for their own presence. Some of the mysterious changes in the abundance of common shore animals may, in time, be firmly linked to such changes in the biological properties of the water around them. And again we seem to be sent back to the larval stages for an understanding of how and when this fateful influence is exerted." (Beinecke papers)

In the book this note seems to reappear as a philosophical position: "In the sea nothing lives to itself. The very water is altered, in its chemical nature and in its capacity for influencing life processes, by the fact that certain forms have lived within it and have passed on to it new substances capable of inducing far-reaching effects. So the present is linked with past and future, and each living thing with all that surrounds it" (*ES*, 37).

Interconnectedness becomes interdependence in the chapter "The Rocky Shore." In her observation of the rock barnacle she again returns to the idea that "the sea is not its enemy"; each species lives for a time, then leaves something behind for another. "When, through the attacks of fish, predatory worms, or snails, or through natural causes, the barnacle's life comes to an end, the shells remain attached to the rocks. These become shelter for many of the minute beings of the shore. Besides the baby periwinkles that regularly live there, the little tide-pool insects often hurry into these shelters if caught by the rising tide. And lower on the shore, or in tide pools, the empty shells are likely to house young anemones, tube worms, or even new generations of barnacles" (*ES*, 55).

Carson sees other animals as adapting to their habitat and creating a harmony with their surroundings. "The limpet is adapted with beautiful precision to the difficult world of the shore. One expects a snail to have a coiled shell; the limpet has instead a flattened cone" (*ES*, 58). This adaptive cone allows the limpet to press itself against the rocks while the water slides over it. The rock and the sea and the limpet are perfectly harmonious, and, once again, "the sea is not the enemy" because there is an adaptive interconnection among all the elements.

This adjustment is seen in other species as well. Carson notes the adaptive interconnection in the tube worm, the mussel, the periwinkle, and numerous other species that live out their lives at the edge of the sea. Of the mussel's existence, Carson marvels, "For every mussel surviving upon the rocks, there must have been millions of larvae who setting forth into the sea had a disastrous end. The system is in delicate balance; barring catastrophe, the forces that destroy neither outweigh nor are outweighed by those that create, and over the years of a man's life, as over the ages of recent geologic time, the total number of mussels on the shore probably has remained about the same" (*ES*, 92). Balance, adjustment, interdependence are all central both to the life of the shore and to Carson's view of the world. And it is in this broader area that Carson witnesses the manifestation of her vision of the world.

The wave-battered rocky coast of Maine seems to be the harshest for intertidal life. As Carson moves south to the sandy beaches of the middle and southern states, she observes that "the sea and the land lie here in a relation established gradually, over millions of years" (*ES*, 125). The contours of the land are softer, created by "the unhurried process of erosion . . . despite the constant working over of the sands by wind and water, a beach shows little visible change from day to day, for as one grain is carried away, another is usually brought to take its place" (*ES*, 126). This view of the simultaneously changeless yet ever-changing nature of the seashore is an important element in Carson's ecological vision. For the time she worked on *The Edge of the Sea*, before she began contemplating *Silent Spring*, she was at peace with a natural world that she felt confident was constantly renewing itself, remaining ever vital and viable. "Barring catastrophe," she writes in *The Edge of the Sea*, the natural world could be relied on to maintain itself. Within three years of the publication of her idyllic shore book, Carson would find that catastrophe.

What Carson calls the "intricate dependence of one species upon another" (*ES*, 151) goes on eternally, and each creature, in its individual life, is like a microcosm of the species and of the throbbing life of the shore. All creatures live out their lives and in death contribute their bodies for others to live: "In the litter of the tide lines they find morsels of dead fish or crab shells containing remnants of flesh; so the beach is cleaned and the phosphates, nitrates, and other mineral substances are recovered from the dead for use by the living" (*ES*, 162).

As Carson walked the beaches of North and South Carolina, she was acutely aware of the way in which life adapts. Asking herself how, when a jetty, a seawall, or a bridge was built, a specific animal happened to be at hand to colonize that structure, she concluded that there was a "ceaseless migration, for the most part doomed to futility, yet ensuring that always, when opportunity arises, life shall be waiting, ready to take advantage. For the ocean currents are not merely a movement of water; they are a stream of life" (*ES*, 189). This "stream of life" is the same one Carson illustrated in "Birth of an Island," in *The Sea around Us*. Just as plant and animal life float in the air, wafted by currents, looking for a place to populate, so creatures of the sea are carried by the currents looking for a place to inhabit.

Carson's and her readers' voyage in *The Edge of the Sea* continues south from the sandy beaches to the coral coast of Florida. This is the only coral coast in the United States, and there is very little to compare with it anywhere else in the world. Carson chose to study the coral coast because it offered a contrast to the rocky coast of New England and the sandy beaches of the mid-Atlantic states. "This is a coast not formed of lifeless rock or sand, but created by the activities of living things which, though having bodies formed of protoplasm even as our own, are able to turn the substance of the sea into rock" (*ES*, 191). The very shore is alive, or once was, and that vitality adds a special dimension to the chapter on the Florida Keys. The coral reefs themselves become the metaphor for Carson's most persistent ideas about the processes of life and about the interconnectedness of land and sea. The coral coast, "in its being and its meaning . . . represents not merely an uneasy equilibrium of land and water masses; it is eloquent of a continuing change now actually in progress, a change being brought about by the life processes of living things" (*ES*, 194).

The interrelations of the creatures of the coral reef reiterate the relationships found between creatures and the intertidal zones further north. The gall crab, for instance, lives within a cavity it has made in the surface of a living brain coral. It moves freely in and out as a young crab, but as it grows, it becomes trapped in the home it has made. Since the male of this species remains tiny, it can move among the imprisoned females. Trapped and provided for, linked inextricably to the brain coral, the gall crab is yet another illustration of how one form of life provides for another.

Even in areas of the tide line where life is generally inhospitable, Carson found plants and animals thriving. One example is the vermitide. This snail, Carson informs her readers, behaves in a most unsnail-like manner. Where most snails are solitary, the vermitides are gregarious colonists; where most roam, the vermitide is sedentary; where most snails hunt and scrape food from the rocks, the vermitide simply draws sea water into its body for and extracts nourishment. Indeed, Carson concludes, "by becoming the imperfect, the atypical snail, they have become the perfectly adapted exploiter of the opportunities of their world" (*ES*, 213).

Carson also observes the mutability of the land and sea themselves, on a small and a grand scale. On the coral coast are changes that a person can witness in a lifetime. The mangrove swamps are a good example: "Today we can see, from one generation of man to another, where several small islands have coalesced to form one, or where the land has grown out and an island has merged with it – sea becoming land almost before our eyes" (*ES,* 246). Just as sea can become land, land can be subsumed by the sea. Carson, standing on the rocky coast of Maine, realizes: "Once this rocky coast beneath me was a plain of sand; then the sea rose and found a new shore line. And again in some shadowy future the surf will have ground these rocks to sand and will have returned the coast to its earlier state. And so in my mind's eye these coastal forms merge and blend in a shifting kaleidoscopic pattern in which there is no finality, no ultimate and fixed reality – earth becoming fluid as the sea itself" (*ES,* 249-50).

Response to the Book

The Edge of the Sea was a best-seller. Reviewers praised the very elements they had praised in her earlier books: scientific accuracy, thoroughgoing curiosity about and reverence for the sea, and her ability to make science into poetry. The book was, said one reviewer, "a flowing account of the interdependence and intricate relationships with one another and with their environment among a host of forms of animal and plant life of the Atlantic littoral."[6] Most reviewers recognized how this book, along with the two preceding it, created a fascination for the sea and enriched its symbolic meaning for readers while heightening their scientific knowledge.

Perhaps one of the most rewarding responses to *The Edge of the Sea* came from a high school student, Susan Teele, who on 13 May 1959 wrote to Carson: "I want to express my sincere appreciation for this wondrous writing. It has contributed a fuller knowledge of the sea, as well as a matchless entertainment. Your writing is truly a thing of beauty and sincerity" (Beinecke papers). Carson responded on 27 May 1959: "Your letter is one of the most rewarding ones I have ever received. I find myself astonished at the thoughts you, at your age, have expressed so clearly and with such perception" (Beinecke papers).

With the publication of three books about the sea, there was a growing interest in Carson herself. In an interview with the *Washington Star,* Carson admitted, with characteristic dry humor, "I don't swim very well . . . I am only mildly enthusiastic about seafoods, and do not keep tropical fish as pets."[7]

A Sense of Wonder

The pleasure Carson took in the years she worked on *The Edge of the Sea* seems to have carried over to her next project, a magazine article for *Woman's Home Companion,* "Help Your Child to Wonder." This short article, published in July 1956, focused on concerns Carson had expressed time and again. She realized that it was difficult for adults caught in the difficult task of providing for their families to take time out to help their children appreciate nature. She also recognized that parents missed things young children noticed. Perhaps because "they themselves are small and closer to the ground than we, [children] notice and delight in the small and inconspicuous."[8] Much of nature is inconspicuous to the inattentive eye, and adults, by sharing time with their children in the natural world, might revive their own sense of wonder in it.

Carson did not believe that parents had to identify "birds, insects, rocks, stars, or any other of the living and nonliving things that share this world with us" (*SW,* 82). Rather she believed that it was much more important for parents to pass on to their children a curiosity and reverence for the natural world. Children would find the terms for what they observed later on.

Carson had hoped to expand the magazine article "Help Your Child to Wonder," into a much larger book. She wrote an outline of it for Marie Rodell, in which she listed "The Sky," "The Woods," "The Sea," "The Changing Year," "The World of Tiny Things," "The Miracle of Life," and "Beauty in Nature" as prospective chapters. When making notes for the book, Carson emphasized: "I would once have discussed only the way the physical world molds life. Now there is a fresh, new theme – how life changes environment" (Beinecke papers).

This intensified concern for the interrelation between the physical world and life was heightened by her research for *Silent Spring.* More and more, as she read document after document about dying birds and stunted flora, she realized the world was changing beyond what she had perceived was possible as a younger scientist. Always a conservationist, she had once thought there were elements of the natural world that could not be violated. While she was working on "Help Your Child to Wonder" and making plans for the book-length version, she had to take into consideration just how much human damage had been done to the environment. Her plans for the longer work were based not simply on the Wordsworthian assumption that children had an innate sense of awe for the processes of the natural world but also on the growing sense of urgency she felt for the world around her. She thought that if children could retain their love of nature into adulthood, perhaps the earth could be saved. The impact that life had on the environment could be mitigated or rendered more benign.

With illness and responsibility dogging her from 1958 until her death, Carson was not to expand the article into a book, although the article was published in book form the year after her death, in 1965. More important, Carson would never again experience the sheer joy of standing in the tide pools, chronicling the lives of the tiny creatures therein. The last six years of her life would present the greatest challenge to her scientific research skills; the task she set for herself of finding and documenting the destructive effects of herbicides and pesticides would consume nearly all of her time and energy.

Chapter Four

Conflict

There is no doubt that *Silent Spring* was "comparable in its impact on public consciousness, and demand for instant action, to Tom Paine's *Common Sense*, Harriet Beecher Stowe's *Uncle Tom's Cabin*, and Upton Sinclair's *The Jungle*."[1] Indeed, *Silent Spring* is a revolutionary document that voices the concerns of many who, after World War II, began to see the technology of war being applied indiscriminately against nature. As James Whorton points out in *Before Silent Spring*, the wartime use of DDT often saved lives: "When Typhus was introduced into Naples in December 1943 dusting stations were established throughout the city, and . . . the incipient epidemic was quelled with no loss of American lives."[2] The shift to a peace economy fostered experimentation with DDT and other chemical agents to control pests – such as the boll weevil, the Colorado potato beetle, and the fire ant – and to contain the spread of vegetation that competed with cash crops.

A letter to Carson from C. J. Briejer, director of the Dutch Plant Pest Control Service, on 2 February 1962 indicates how DDT went from savior to destroyer in a short period of time. He recalls the Netherlands in 1944 as "a big concentration camp. . . . People were extremely weakened by lack of food. . . . Fleas and body lice were abundant . . . some pockets of fever already in existence. In that situation DDT was a blessing. . . . It is doubtful whether the Allies could have taken the risk of an invasion without DDT." Briejer went on to recount that all the crops were also "seriously infested with insects. Our potato fields were teeming with Colorado beetles. There again DDT was the answer. Much of the quick recovering of Western Europe was due to DDT. . . . I realize that I probably would not live and write to you today if in 1944 no powerful insecticide had been available." He goes on to say that while DDT was "a blessing" in 1944, it was "a very temporary blessing," which could "in rather a short time . . . turn into a curse." Briejer concludes, "We are going to have to do some very energetic research on other control measures, measures that will have to be biological, not chemical. Our aim should be to guide natural processes as cautiously as possible in the desired direction rather than to use brute force" (Beinecke papers).

The Years before *Silent Spring*

Prior to World War II various methods had been employed to control pests and unwanted plants. Many of these compounds were arsenic derivatives, and while they might have been effective against pests, they also endangered livestock or farmers who were careless in their application of the compounds. Furthermore, as Whorton points out, "honey bees would be vulnerable to insecticides" (Whorton, 27). As with DDT in the 1950s and 1960s, there was a history of controversy over the use of arsenic compounds in insecticides prior to World War II. Many farmers used the compounds, such as Paris Green and London Purple, indiscriminately, while bee keepers and entomologists warned of the dangers. Indeed, in their attempt to control unwanted insects on their farms, farmers used anything with any degree of potency. As late as 1951, Carson writes, the British Ministry of Agriculture warned of "the hazards of going into the arsenic sprayed fields, but the warning was not understood by the cattle . . . and reports of cattle poisoned by the arsenic sprays came with monotonous regularity."[3]

The same laxness about health and safety prevailed when DDT went on the market: "The forester sprayed to protect his trees, the cranberry picker to protect his bogs, the cotton planter to save his cotton from the boll weevil, and so on down a long procession of farmers and gardeners – with little or no understanding of or concern for the consequences" (Downs, 261). Dubbed the "atomic bomb of the insect world" (Whorton, 249), DDT's postwar history was anything but salutary. Despite the Department of Agriculture's unreserved support, there were some who believed a detailed study of the long-term effects of the miracle chemical was necessary.

Clarence Cottam was concerned with the Department of Agriculture's position, as was Carson herself. Both continued to research the effects of chlorinated hydrocarbons – the active ingredient in DDT and related pesticides. Shortly after the war Carson proposed an article to *Reader's Digest* about the deleterious effects of DDT and was turned down. While more than a decade would pass before Carson turned her complete attention to the topic, this early query to *Reader's Digest* does indicate how long-standing her concerns were. In the letter, Carson wrote, "We have all heard a lot about what DDT will soon do for us by wiping out insect pests. The experiments at Patuxent [a research refuge of the U.S. Fish and Wildlife Service in Bowie, Maryland] have been planned to show what other effects DDT may have if applied to wide areas: what it will do to insects that are beneficial or even essential; how it may affect waterfowl, or birds that depend on insect food; whether it may upset the whole delicate balance of nature if unwisely used" (Brooks, 229). At the same time Edwin Way Teale also warned: "A spray as indiscriminate as DDT can upset the economy of nature as much as a revolution upsets social economy" (Brooks, 230-31).

Carson, Cottam, Teale, and others like them raised their concerns to deaf ears. The mid-1940s were a heady time for the United States. It had defeated the Axis powers and was the only major power in the world not devastated by the war. It was in a position to take charge of the future. Many plans involved solidifying America's hegemony by making it the indisputable food supplier for the world. DDT would, according to the Department of Agriculture, make those plans a reality. Farmers saw DDT as a final solution to pests, a guarantee of increased crop yields and larger profits. The Department of Agriculture promoted that view and, despite the appearance of articles about the dangers of DDT as early as 1945 in *Harper's* and the *Atlantic Monthly*, (Brooks, 230), the world at large was prepared to spray, spray, spray.

Between the end of the war and 1957, Carson continued to track the use of DDT and other powerful toxic chemicals used in pesticides and weed killers. She corresponded with her friend and fellow scientist Clarence Cottam, who was now director of the Welder Wildlife Foundation in Texas, about the controversial fire ant program sponsored by the Department of Agriculture. Fire ants, indigenous to South America, had come into the United States on ships docking in Mobile Bay. While the ants could not be completely eliminated, they had been contained fairly easily in colonies in Alabama, Louisiana, and Texas. The Department of Agriculture moved aggressively to eliminate the insect on the grounds that it destroyed crops such as cotton and beans, endangered wildlife, and even posed a direct threat to human beings.

A pamphlet disseminated by the Department of Agriculture said that "Chlordane, dieldrin, and aldrin are the best insecticides to use for controlling imported fire ants" ("Facts about Imported Fire Ant Program," Beinecke papers). While the pamphlet does warn that the chemicals are poisons and should be used with caution, there is little indication of their real potency. DDT, chlordane, dieldrin, and aldrin are also members of a group of organic synthetic insecticides that do not break down in the environment but tend to be recycled through food chains.[4] W. H. Drinkard, director of the Alabama Department of Conservation, had warned in the May 1958 issue of *Nature Conservation News* that treatments of fire ant mounds with heptachlor, another USDA recommended chemical, "may kill up to 75 percent of the bird and game populations within the first two weeks after application" (Beinecke papers).

What finally turned Carson from observer to activist, however, was not the fire ant program but a court trial in Long Island, New York, and a letter to the editor in a Boston newspaper from a bird watcher. The trial was the result of work by Robert Cushman Murphy and Marjorie Spock, who brought suit against the State of New York and the federal government for aerial spraying of DDT to control the gypsy moth. When Spock learned through Marie Rodell of Carson's interest in the long-term effects of pesticides on human beings and animals, she began to send Carson clippings about the effects of spraying on bird mortality.

The letter from the bird watcher, Olga Owens Huckins of Duxbury, Massachusetts, described what happened to birds on her property after DDT had been sprayed to eliminate mosquitoes. Huckins noted that the so-called "harmless" shower of DDT spray "killed seven of our lovely song-birds outright." Her letter went on to describe the deaths of other birds in her yard and in the marsh near her house: "All the birds died horribly and in the same way. Their bills were gaping open, and their splayed claws were drawn up to their breasts in agony" (Brooks, 232; first printed in the *Boston Herald*, 29 January 1958). Huckins's letter also rebutted the arguments made by some who claimed that it was better to have DDT than to have mosquitoes: "All summer long, every time we went into the garden, we were attacked by the most voracious mosquitoes that had ever appeared there. But the grasshoppers, visiting bees, and other harmless insects, were all gone" (Brooks, 232). Huckins then sent a copy of her letter to Carson with an inquiry about which agencies in the government she could appeal to in order to prevent the spraying of DDT.

Huckins's inquiry and Carson's correspondence with Marjorie Spock and Robert Cushman Murphy about the evidence being used in the New York trial heavily contributed to her decision to write a *Silent Spring.*

Researching Pesticides

Carson was eminently suited to the task of writing *Silent Spring.* Her meticulous research methods, developed over the years she was writing the books about the sea, served her in the very difficult task of compiling information about the damage that chlorinated hydro-carbons were doing to the environment. Her files also reveal that she was not simply interested in the effects of pesticides; rather, she was concerned with the way people were living in their world and what was happening to them as a result of careless environmental policies. Carson pursued several avenues of investigation at one time. She kept a file of clippings, articles, and book references on topics such as radiation and atomic pollution, causes of cancer, food additives, air pollution, and the fire ant program. She was concerned about how pesticides poisoned the food we eat, the air we breathe, and the water we drink. Her files also show that Carson was concerned about smog, radioactive fallout, and other forms of air pollution.

During the late 1950s the *New Yorker* had a weekly column called "These Precious Days" – the magazine's "fever chart of the planet Earth, showing Man's ups and downs in contaminating the air, the sea and the soil." Carson collected these columns and noted the rise in Strontium 90 indicated there in vegetables. She commented twice that vegetables absorbed more Strontium 90 than grasses or milk from grazing milk cows. Further, she kept notes on bone cancers from fallout from weapons tested in the early 1950s.

Her files on the use of chlorinated hydrocarbons to control the imported fire ants contained the findings, published in 1959, of a five-year study on insect control called "Residual Effectiveness of Chlorinated Hydrocarbons for Control of the Imported Fire Ant."

The study concluded that "when broadcast treatment lost effectiveness, the number of mounds per acre was greater than on the untreated areas" (Beinecke papers). Carson also recorded in the same yeard that Texas Game and Fish biologists "noted heavy wildlife losses from heptachlor treatment of the imported fire ant" (Beinecke papers).

At the 12th Annual Conference of the Southeastern Section of the Wildlife Society in 1959, Cottam pointed out that the fire ant program had resulted in significant losses of domestic animals as well as wildlife. With regard to bird populations, which first brought the problem of chemical spraying to Carson's attention, Cottam noted: "Laboratory experiments found that these highly toxic chlorinated hydrocarbons not only are extremely lethal in minute quantities but that these poisons are accumulative and that young birds hatched from parents that had ingested minute sub-lethal doses of poison showed a much higher mortality after hatching and that sterility or partial sterility often follows in those young that do survive" (Beinecke papers).

In direct contradiction to studies conducted by the University of Michigan, Michigan State University, the University of Wisconsin, and the Patuxent Research Refuge were a barrage of pamphlets from the U.S. Department of Agriculture, which insisted that, with precautions, the use of DDT would have no adverse effects on human beings or on wildlife. Among the recommended precautions was to "avoid inhaling the dusts or sprays." Physicians, meanwhile, were insisting that medical personnel wear protective clothing and masks even when handling the clothing of those poisoned by insecticides.

Another story that came to light around this time on the abuse of pesticides was the cranberry scare. During Thanksgiving and Christmas of 1959 cranberries were contaminated by the weed killer aminotriazole, then a known carcinogen. Arthur S. Fleming, secretary of the Department of Health, Education, and Welfare, touched off a controversy when he recommended that the use of aminotriazole in connection with cranberry growing be banned. In keeping with its policy "not to permit the use of chemicals in food when it is established that they cause cancer in animals or in man,"[5] the Food and Drug Administration had earlier refused to set a tolerance level on aminotriazole and had also recommended a ban; the FDA's refusal to set a level indicated its belief that there was no level at which amino-triazole could be viewed as "safe."

Fleming's recommendation publicized the issue and brought it to a head, triggering a strong reaction from agricultural interests. The 1 February 1960 *New York Times* noted that "eleven major farm organizations – embodying essentially the massive political might of the entire farm bloc – went to the White House and, in effect, demanded that President Eisenhower repudiate Mr. Fleming." Lloyd Bentsen, then secretary of the Department of Agriculture, acted in the farmers' behalf and tried to overrule Fleming's recommendation. The *Washington Post* noted on 5 February 1960 that farmers had been violating the Food and Drug Act regularly by using forbidden pesticides.

A study conducted by the FDA in Texas in 1960 found evidence of pesticide abuse in the dairy industry. One of the top U.S. food and drug policing officials disclosed that one third of all manufactured dairy products that had been sampled over a period of several months contained noticeable amounts of pesticide. The official said the finding was potentially more explosive than the cranberry scare (Beinecke papers). Carson was particularly concerned about increasing concentrations of toxins as they moved up the food chain. Her notes quote Robert B. Dinley, Jr., from the Denver Wildlife Research Center record: "So far we know almost nothing about the possible accumulation of DDT in deer and in other game animals and the possible effects of these residues on the game species and on the hunters that eat the game" (Beinecke papers). This sense that the damage human beings inflicted on the natural world would come back to them goes to the heart of *Silent Spring.*

Of even deeper and likely more personal concern to Carson – who had been diagnosed with cancer in 1957, treated again in 1958, given a radical mastectomy in 1960, and treated continually for the disease until her death in 1964 – was the link between toxic chemicals such as DDT and cancer. Carson's files were beginning to tell a tale of the long-range effects of DDT. She began keeping files of articles on causes, incidences, and locations of cancers for her research on *Silent Spring,* including the work of W. C. Hueper. As early as 1948 Hueper had related chlorinated hydrocarbons to the incidence of cancer and written about environmental and occupational cancers.[6] In a 1957 pamphlet Hueper wrote for the American

Medical Association, he noted that human beings were "increasingly exposed to new harmful inanimate agents against which [they] neither possess adequate natural defense mechanisms nor [have] sufficient time to develop them through natural or artificial pro- cesses . . . the fact that malignancy has not (as yet) been reported among livestock feeding on vegetation treated with weed killers means little or nothing, for seldom are such animals permitted to live out the period of years necessary for cancer to develop."[7] Carson initialed a comment Hueper made about the need for careful study of weed killers as "cancer hazards to man."

Malcom Hargraves of the Mayo Clinic, who in 1959 testified in Long Island in behalf of Murphy and Spock against the widespread spraying of gypsy moths, stated at the trial that the majority of the hematologists associated with him at the Mayo Clinic shared his views on the toxicity of pesticides and their effect on human health. "In my mind," he said, "I am positive that these [aplastic anemias, lymphomas, and leukemias] are due to exposure to environmenal agents" (Beinecke papers). The Long Island case eventually went as far as the U.S. Supreme Court, which on 28 March 1960 refused to overturn the appeals court decision against plaintiffs Murphy and Spock. Chief Justice William O. Douglas, citing "the great public importance" of the issues involved in the case, dissented from the majority opinion (Beinecke papers).

Even with the masses of seemingly overwhelming evidence of the environmental chaos caused by the uncontrolled use of pesticides, Carson had a long way to go to convince the public. In *Silent Spring*, she had to relate to her reader in a coherent form the concept of the interconnectedness of life, just as she had in her three books about the sea.

The Book

Silent Spring is, quite simply, a plea for reason and balance in the use of pesticides. But more than that, it is a beautifully structured and well-written book. Like Carson's three previous books, it is a masterpiece of scientific accuracy couched in the language of the poet. All of her books about the sea play variations on the same theme: nature is a delicate series of interconnections that over the millennia, prior to human intervention, have created a perfect synthesis. In *Silent Spring* Carson shifts her focus precisely to that human intervention.

The book opens with a fable, the story of a town "in the heart of America where all life seemed to live in harmony with its surroundings" (*SS*, 1). The picture Carson paints is of an idyllic rural town in America's heartland, but the idyll is destroyed: "Some evil spell had settled on the community. . . . Everywhere was the shadow of death" (*SS*, 2). In the opening chapter of *Silent Spring*, Carson seems to be remembering her own childhood – the walks in the woods, the family's orchards. She may also be remembering the blight that came to Springdale with industrial pollution.

The parable of the happy valley introduces the reader to the chilling possibilities for destruction that are outlined in the text. Carson does not simply catalog the problems caused by pesticides but shows how they are indicative of a new and pernicious way of looking at the world. In fact, what Carson recognized in the years after World War II was that the human relationship to the planet had changed. "Only within the moment of time represented by the present century has one species – man – acquired significant power to alter the nature of his world. During the past quarter century this power has not only increased to one of disturbing magnitude but it has changed in character" (*SS*, 5-6). What Carson points out early in *Silent Spring* is that pesticide pollution is not an aberration, it is the newest and perhaps "the most alarming of all man's assaults upon the environment" (*SS*, 6). This new attack (polluting the air, earth, and soil with chemicals and radioactive waste) created a chain of poisoning and death that would imperil human beings as well as the natural world, for "the chemical war is never won, and all life is caught in its violent crossfire" (*SS*, 8).

Structurally, Carson works cyclically from water to earth to air and around again. As she begins with the surface waters and the underground seas, Carson is truly in her element. If "water is life," it is also death. The same connectedness and interdependence that make life possible – and that Carson celebrated in her earlier books – also lead to its destruction. "It is not possible to add pesticides to water anywhere without threatening the purity of water everywhere," Carson maintains. "Seldom if ever does Nature operate in closed and separate compartments, and she has not done so in distributing the earth's water supply . . . all the running water of the earth's surface was at one time groundwater. And so in a very real and frightening sense, pollution of the groundwater is pollution of water everywhere" (*SS*, 42).

The process of pollution is a dark and terrifying one, Carson illustrates: "it must have been by such a dark, underground sea that poisonous chemicals traveled from a manufacturing plant in Colorado to a farming district several miles away, there to poison wells, sicken humans and livestock, and damage crops" (*SS*, 42).

More important even than the process of the spread of pollution by groundwater is the idea that the chlorinated hydrocarbons become increasingly concentrated as they move from one part of nature's chain to the next. Carson uses the example of Clear Lake in California to highlight the phenomenon. Clear Lake was sprayed with DDD, "a close relative of DDT" (*SS*, 46), to control gnats. Within the year, the western grebe, a bird that winters and breeds in Clear Lake, began to die. While there was no longer an indication that DDD was present in the water, Carson writes, "the poison had not really left the lake; it had merely gone into the fabric of the life the lake supports" (*SS*, 48). The poison passed from generation to generation of the plankton in the lake, into the fish, the frogs, and finally the grebes. Carson notes that while the concentration in the lake was minimal and quickly disappeared, that in the plankton was "25 times the maximum concentration ever reached in the water itself" (*SS*, 48). The amount of DDD in the flesh of fish and frogs, "always exceeded by many times the original concentration in the water" (*SS*, 48). And on and on until it reached the grebe, which it killed.

On the Miramichi River in New Brunswick millions of young salmon died after the aerial spraying of evergreens to stop budworm infestation. This scene of devastation was repeated over and over again: aerial spraying, clouds of pesticides settling on the ground to be washed into streams and rivers, millions of dead fish. It happened in Yellowstone National Park; it happened in British Columbia, Louisiana, Alabama, Florida, Texas, Oklahoma, Chesapeake Bay – the trail of death continued.

"In nature," Carson reminds the reader, "nothing exists alone" (*SS*, 51). If the water is polluted, the earth is going to be as well. While no DDD was found in Clear Lake shortly after its application, its by-products persisted in the soil. "Aldrin [was] recovered after four years," Carson reports, "both as traces and more abundantly as converted to dieldrin" (*SS*, 58). Even the tobacco in cigarettes that many smoked as they read Carson's book contained persistent poisons that had leached into the soil. Arsenic, the old prechlorinated hydrocarbon stand-by, permanently poisons the soil. The arsenic content of cigarettes made from American tobacco "*increased more than 300 per cent* between the years 1932 and 1952" (*SS*, 58; Carson's italics). Even baby food manufacturers had reason to be concerned about soil contamination, Carson writes. "This very sort of contamination has created endless problems for at least one leading manufacturer of baby foods who has been unwilling to buy any fruits or vegetables on which toxic insecticides have been used" (*SS*, 59).

It is in her chapter "Earth's Green Mantle" that the reasonableness of Carson's concerns becomes apparent. In it, she addresses the broadcast – or undirected – spraying of roadsides to eliminate flora that obstructs driver vision. Spraying programs in Maine, Connecticut, Massachusetts, and other New England states demonstrated improper planning and massive abuse. Uncontrolled spraying left dead cows and scorched earth in its wake, where previously "nature's own landscape [had] provided a border of alder, viburnum, sweet fern, and juniper with seasonally changing accents of bright flowers or of fruits hanging in jeweled clusters" (*SS*, 71). Such destruction is not only spatial, Carson argues, but temporal: not just one but several generations of flowers would be lost in New England. If nature, without human interference, can create a "material immortality," human beings can, in one short season, guarantee destruction far into the future.

To redress the problem Carson did not suggest an all-out ban but selective spraying, an idea that made scientific and economic sense. The process, developed by Frank Egler, was very simple. It took into consideration that the destruction of roadside shrubbery would lead to an invasion of grasses that were not resistant to the regrowth of trees that obstructed vision. It also, as Carson notes, "took advantage of the inherent stability of nature, building on the fact that most communities of shrubs are strongly resistant to invasion by trees" (*SS*, 74).

Where selective spraying, the process of targeting specific trees and spraying their bases, has been adopted, "an area becomes stabilized, *requiring no respraying for at least 20 years*" (*SS*, 75; Carson's italics). Her appeal to the taxpayer was simple: "When taxpayers understand that the bill for spraying the town roads should come due only once a generation instead of once a year, they will surely rise up and demand a change of method" (SS, 75). Indeed, that is just what many began to do; they sought injunctions against broadcast spraying and, in some cases, actually sued their local governments when spraying continued.

Carson also wrote about the effects of broadcast spraying on air quality. Like radiation (Carson makes the comparison time and again), toxic residues drift silently on air currents and fall on unsuspecting and unprotected human beings as well as on target insects or plants. Carson's chilling documentation of aerial spraying in the city of Detroit to rid the area of Japanese beetles not only revealed the carelessness of the procedure but also the indifference of officials who should have been aware of the dangers. Both the Federal Aviation Agency and the Detroit Department of Parks and Recreation assured worried citizens that "the dust is harmless to humans and will not hurt plants or pets" (SS, 89). Carson describes the spraying: "The pellets of insecticide fell on beetles and humans alike, showers of 'harmless' poison descending on people shopping or going to work and on children out from school for the lunch hour. Housewives swept the granules from porches and sidewalks, where they are said to have 'looked like snow'" (SS, 90).

The effect of this indiscriminate "safe" spraying was "a great many dead and dying birds." Carson continues: "A local veterinarian reported that his office was full of clients with dogs and cats that had suddenly sickened. Cats, who so meticulously groom their coats and lick their paws, seem to be the most affected" (SS, 90). The same problem occurred in Illinois, where beetle spraying also took place. Carson noted that in one area of Illinois that was sprayed repeatedly and indiscriminately, there was hardly a farm that had a cat. Carson concluded that "Incidents like the eastern Illinois spraying raise a question that is not only scientific but moral. The question is whether any civilization can wage relentless war on life without destroying itself, and without losing the right to be called civilized" (SS, 99).

Carson threw down the gauntlet with that question. In her earlier books Carson had highlighted the need to conserve and protect the oceans, but, as H. Patricia Hynes points out, the purpose of those books "was not a worldly call to stop polluting the sea. Rather those books stirred people to love the sea because of its beauty for which she was their eyes, for its mystery of which she was the oracle, and for its cadence and sound for which she was its voice" (Hynes, 35). The purpose of *Silent Spring*, while Carson was the eyes, oracle, and voice of the beauty, order, and cadences of nature, was quite simply to get people to stop pollution. The first line of attack was pointing out the destruction of human habitations; the second was highlighting the cost to consumers and the profits to big business. The third line of argument was the moral one: human beings have an obligation not to destroy the world in which they and other species live even if their scientific knowledge has given them the means to do so. That last argument was Carson's most enduring, and it was the argument that pitted her squarely against those who refused to acknowledge the damage being done by pesticides.

Carson felt the loss of birds to pesticides deeply. The fate of the robin, in particular, came to symbolize for her the plight of the natural world. The robin's fate was tied inextricably to the fate of the elm and the lowly earthworm. It was Dutch elm disease that brought the tree into the Department of Agriculture's spraying program, and it was that program that so devastated the robin, whose major source of food is the earthworm, which processes fallen leaves. The worms acted as "magnifiers" of DDT, and that magnification killed the robins outright or rendered them sterile. It was indeed a silent spring when no robin sang.

Over time, Carson noted that birds were not only the incidental target for spraying, dropping by the hundreds as they landed in sprayed trees, made their nests of sprayed grasses, or ate worms and other insects contaminated with pesticides; birds became, when farmers found them irksome, the direct target. "There is a growing trend toward aerial applications of such deadly poisons as parathion to 'control' concentrations of birds distasteful to farmers" (*SS*, 126). Another government agency, the Fish and Wildlife Service, expressed serious concern over the blanket use of pesticides to control nature for the benefit of farmers. In Indiana, for example, 65,000 red-winged blackbirds were killed in 1957 by a single application of parathion. Unfortunately "parathion is not a specific for blackbirds: it is a universal killer" (*SS*, 126).

With the destruction of birds in such enormous numbers, Carson had to ask, "Who has made the decision that sets in motion these chains of poisonings, this ever-widening wave of death that spreads out, like ripples when a pebble is dropped into a still pond? Who has placed in one pan of the scales the leaves that might have been eaten by the beetles and in the other the pitiful heaps of many-hued feathers, the lifeless remains of the birds that fell before the unselective bludgeon of insecticidal poisons? Who has decided – who has the right to decide – for the countless legions of people who were not consulted that the supreme value is a world without insects, even though it be also a sterile world ungraced by the curving wing of a bird in flight?" (SS, 127).

Carson's anger builds as the chapters reveal scene after scene of devastation; her outrage crescendoes in "Beyond the Dreams of the Borgias." The title is a fitting gloss on Carson's attitude toward wanton destruction of the environment. The Borgia family, political figures in late fifteenth- and early sixteenth-century Italy renowned for poisoning their enemies, is for Carson emblematic of big business and government in the twentieth century – except that plants, fish, birds, and other human beings are the random victims of a misdirected war against nature. Carol Gartner points out that Carson's use of language throughout the book highlights the thematic idea of "pesticide used as warfare" (Gartner, 99). Words such as "chemical war," "crusade," "allies and enemies, "weapons, "lethal power," and "explosive power" hammer home the metaphor that we are engaged in a war against nature that will inevitably destroy us as well as our supposed enemies.

Carson returns repeatedly to the image of the Borgias. Their war, too, was more subtle and secretive than the outright violence of pitched battles. She recounts the "innumerable small-scale exposures to which we are subjected day by day, year after year" (SS, 173). In fact, she writes, "to find a diet free from DDT and related chemicals it seems one must go to a remote and primitive land, still lacking the amenities of civilization" (SS, 179). When we sit down to dinner, she suggests, we may be "in little better position than the guests of the Borgias" (SS, 184). Even more disturbing is the threat of delayed effects from toxic substances. When we cross beyond the point of no return, she believed, we won't know it for perhaps another 20 years (SS, 188).

Here Carson enters new territory, the "ecology of the world within our bodies. In this unseen world minute causes produce mighty effects; the effect, moreover, is often seemingly unrelated to the cause, appearing in a part of the body remote from the area where the original injury was sustained" (*SS*, 189). Cancer, sterility, and birth defects, Carson argued, could result from the silent intrusion of human cells by pesticides and the by-products of their breakdown. While this cause-and-effect relationship between certain toxic chemicals and cellular damage is today generally acknowledged, this was not the case more than 30 years ago, when *Silent Spring* was published. Carson was among the first scientists to assimilate research from disparate sources to focus on the links between pesticides and cancer.

Put very simply, Carson viewed the body's cellular response to toxic substances as being parallel to that of the natural world. The intrusion of these substances throws a well-functioning system out of control – not just one cog or wheel in the system, but its entire balance and function. In attempting to take control of the natural world, human beings, she believed, had lost sight of two important factors: that "the really effective control of insects is that applied by nature not by man" and that "the truly explosive power of a species to reproduce once the resistance of the environment has been weakened" cannot be stopped by human beings (*SS*, 247). In these two points Carson articulates the whole problem of pesticides in much the same way that she was able to articulate the delicate balance of life in the sea. Nature can control insect pests that threaten the balance of life on the planet as long as human beings do not compromise the natural ability of the system to do so. And therein lies the problem. The introduction of pesticides weakened nature's own capacity to balance and control insect populations.

In explaining the careful husbandry of nature, Carson once again returns to her favorite metaphor, the sea, and relates that metaphor to our life on earth: "We see the miracle of nature's control at work when the cod move through winter seas to their spawning grounds, where each female deposits several millions of eggs. The sea does not become a solid mass of cod as it would surely do if all the progeny of all the cod were to survive. The checks that exist in nature are such that out of the millions of young produced by each pair only enough, on the average, survive to adulthood to replace the parent fish" (*SS*, 247-48). The same is true of insects. There is a delicate balance, a great chain of eating and being eaten that keeps both the creatures of the sea and the land in balance. More than simply upsetting the balance of the natural world, the continued and uncontrolled spraying of pesticides could result in the trading of an inconvenient insect for a much more destructive one. Carson again cites the cases of the fire ant program in the South and the Japanese beetle-spraying program in the Midwest. The destruction of the annoying but generally not too harmful fire ant led to an explosion in the population of the sugarcane borer, "one of the worst enemies of the sugarcane crop" (*SS*, 255). The eradication of the Japanese beetle in Illinois left farmers with infestations of corn borers, so, as Carson points out, the farmers "made a poor bargain" (*SS*, 255).

Carson does not simply catalog and list the incidents of insect infestation resulting from thoughtless or irresponsible spraying. She makes an important point about the nature of the world in which we live, and again it is the message of the books about the sea: that all life is interconnected and that the cycles of nature are repeated endlessly in a form of "material immortality." If nature cannot produce a certain number of Japanese beetles to eat the corn borer, or a certain number of fire ants to control the sugarcane borer, or ladybugs to check the spread of spider mites, then these other insects will enjoy population explosions, just as cancer cells, when given the right environment, will overpower normal cells in the human body. Nature will continue to produce life, but with the interference of pesticides, the insect life that is produced might appear more like a cancer than a carefully balanced and regulated harmony of interconnected species living and dying in a naturally regulated pattern. In a note to herself on the book, Carson set up the following schema: "nature out of balance – destruction of food chains – disruption of predator-prey relationships – outbreaks of pest species following spraying – attraction of new pest species into vacuum created by spraying – disturbances of the 'internal ecology' of organism." (Beinecke papers). Thus the cycle of life that Carson had so meticulously researched and illustrated in her earlier books becomes the cycle of death and destruction in *Silent Spring*.

But Carson does not give up on our ability to turn this cycle around. She saw two paths open to people: the one traveled in the years following World War II, laid out by the desire to control nature, and the new one she encouraged her readers to follow, guided by the desire to help nature control itself. In one simple

example of how nature could be helped, Carson reminds readers
that birds, if encouraged, can control many unwanted or harmful
pests. The destruction of forests meant the concomitant destruction
of birds' natural habitat; Carson recommended that bird boxes and
nesting places be constructed to encourage the return of birds to
certain areas.

It is in helping nature help itself to strengthen its defenses
against harmful species that human beings would find an answer to
their problems with certain pests, Carson believe, and begin to live
more in harmony with the world. Preserving and strengthening the
natural world rather than assaulting it with chemicals is the only
lasting solution to the problem. Pesticides might well kill the target
insect, but usually only for a short time. The price paid for that brief
respite from the mosquito, the fire ant, the gypsy moth, or the
Japanese beetle is high. Paradoxically, as Carson notes, the fabric of
life is "on the one hand delicate and destructible, on the other
miraculously tough and resilient, and capable of striking back in
unexpected ways" (*SS*, 297). Human beings have torn the delicate
parts of the fabric, killing the robin, the eagle, the salmon, and even,
if we can admit it, ourselves. What has been gained? In some cases,
"monster" insects that are resistant to the chemicals that have
wreaked such havoc on other parts of the natural world. Nature is
both delicate and resilient, but what is the most delicate is rarely the
most resilient.

Carson saw in the new chemical war against the world an arrogance that is at the root of human beings' relationship with nature.
"The 'control of nature' is a phrase conceived in arrogance, born of
the Neanderthal age of biology and philosophy, when it was supposed that nature exists for the convenience of man. The concepts
and practices of applied entomology for the most part date from that
Stone Age of science. It is our alarming misfortune that so primitive a
science has armed itself with the most modern and terrible weapons,
and that in turning them against the insects it has also turned them
against the earth" (*SS*, 297).

After *Silent Spring*

Immediate reaction to *Silent Spring* was volcanic. Serialized in the
New Yorker beginning in June 1962, the selections were attacked

vociferously and maliciously. Paul Brooks points out that the reaction was intense not simply because Carson questioned the use and abuse of power by certain prominent interest groups but because she questioned the basic attitudes of our technological society toward the natural world. He commented: "The facts she revealed were bad enough, but it was the point of view behind them that was really dangerous and must be suppressed" (Brooks, 293-94).

Chemical companies such as Velsicol Chemical Corporation of Chicago tried to bully Houghton Mifflin into suppressing the book before publication, and agricultural and trade journals went on the attack before the book went on sale. On the basis of the *New Yorker* serialization, Carson was discounted as a "hysterical woman," and there were various parodies, satires, and other attempts to discredit Carson and her findings from such sources as *American Agriculturist, Chemical and Engineering News,* Monsanto Chemical Company, and oddly enough, the Nutrition Foundation of New York City (Brooks, 296). It seems that the Nutrition Foundation received support from university laboratories which were, in turn, heavily endowed by the chemical industry. Carson's theory of interconnectedness is seen in its most unpleasant manifestation in the symbiotic relationship between industry, government, and educational institutions.

Carson was well aware that her assault on the use of pesticides would not be welcomed in many circles. In her letters to colleagues about the book she repeatedly acknowledged that she would have to support every statement with two or three authorities. She had seen how the Department of Agriculture had responded to attempts to control the use of pesticides, and she knew from her experience with the Long Island pesticide trial on the spraying of gypsy moths that to move either government or industry would take a good deal of work.

Clarence Cottam had already warned her, when he read part of a draft of the book, that she would "be subjected to ridicule and condemnation by a few" (Graham, 36). It is doubtful she could have prepared, however, for the vitriolic campaign that ensued. Perhaps the most frustrating aspect of the attacks was that not many of the attackers had done Carson the courtesy of actually reading her book. A quote from the Bethlehem, Pennsylvania, *Globe-Times* captured the mood: "No one in either county farm office who was talked to today had read the book, but all disapproved of it heartily" (Graham,

48). Graham goes on to cite incident after incident of personal attack when the book itself could not be dismissed. A government official queried, "I thought she was a spinster. What's she so worried about genetics for?" (Graham, 49). Attacks that made false claims were particularly difficult to fend off. How often could Carson reiterate, "It is not my contention that chemical insecticides must never be used" (*SS*, 12).

Carson's discussion of roadside spraying should have alerted any sensible reader to the fact that she was not advocating wholesale elimination of the use of chemical controls; she was pleading for responsible use. Apparently, the Department of Agriculture and chemical manufacturers were opposed to any philosophy of pesticide use that did not give them total control. Time and again Carson had to point out that the world she wanted to live in was not a world without synthetic chemicals but a world in which the use of those chemicals was carefully monitored and controlled. Pesticides had become modern-day Frankensteins, monsters beyond the control of the scientists who had invented them.

Because chemical companies had a great deal to lose if Carson's book were taken seriously, they enlisted other groups to spread their message. As Graham points out, they threatened to withdraw advertising from magazines and newspapers that reviewed *Silent Spring* favorably, they gave doctors information kits to help them allay patients' fears about chemical poisoning, and they enlisted the powerful Nutrition Foundation to put together a rebuttal to *Silent Spring*. Ironically, it was partly because of the myriad of biased, distorted attacks that the book gained more committed support from those who found it valuable. Carson's popularity as a writer also made the book difficult to dismiss; instead it attracted a large and international audience.

One result of the widespread interest in the book was CBS's "The *Silent Spring* of Rachel Carson," originally broadcast on 3 April 1963. Hosted by Eric Sevareid and Jay L. McMullen, the program put Carson on television with Robert White-Stevens, the spokesperson for American Cyanamid Corporation. White-Stevens asserted that "the major claims in Miss Rachel Carson's book, *Silent Spring*, are gross distortions of the actual facts, completely unsupported by scientific experimental evidence and general practical experience in the field."[8] Both he and Orville Freeman, the secretary of the

Department of Agriculture, contended that food quality and yields would decline and that the cost of food would rise if pesticides were more tightly controlled. The surgeon general, Luther Terry, cited the control of malaria as evidence of the beneficial use of pesticides, and an apologetic organic farmer said that he couldn't grow as much fruit as his neighbor who used chemical pesticides.

None of the panelists could cite a specific instance of inaccuracy in Carson's book, but White-Stevens continued the chemical manufacturers' general assertion that "there are a number of scientific errors, misquotations, and obvious misinterpretations in her book." He also asserted that, while Carson's material was "in part at least, scientifically accurate," the problem was one of "misplaced emphasis. . . . She discounts and deliberately depreciates all those safety measures which research laboriously has developed and built into each new agricultural chemical that emerges, while she concomitantly builds the possible and alleged hazards of these compounds to horrible and simply staggering dimensions" ("CBS Reports," 11).

The CBS program highlighted the real achievement of Carson's book: despite the negative press it got from many sources, it called attention to the problem of pesticides. Orville Freeman said on the program that people would not want to know they might be facing health hazards. Carson, however, said that if people were made aware of the problem, they would try to act responsibly or at least try to protect themselves from exposure to toxic chemicals. The impression left by the program was that Carson was indeed a level-headed scientist who knew of what she wrote.

In 1981 Bill Moyers re-aired the program and asked Barry Commoner, scientist, author, and environmental activist, to comment on the state of the environment at the time. Commoner responded that even Carson could not have foreseen such disasters as New York's Love Canal, where the dumping of tons of chemical wastes eventually forced the evacuation of an entire community.

While Carson was not alive to hear Commoner's somewhat despairing views of the environment in the 1980s, she was truly pleased with President Kennedy's Science Advisory Committee, which, against the wishes of the Department of Agriculture, wrote a very strong report in 1963 based in large part on her book and her testimony. It went even further than simply condemning government control programs. It mandated that many government agencies, such as the Department of Health, Education, and Welfare, the Department of the Interior, and the Department of Agriculture, rethink their pesticide-related programs and that all agencies keep the public apprised of the decisions made regarding pesticide use and monitoring. One recommendation that "elimination of persistent toxic pesticides should be the goal" must have pleased Carson immensely. Carson's aims in writing *Silent Spring* – to alert the public and "to build a fire under the Government" (Graham, 79) – seemed to have been achieved.

Chapter Five

Carson and the Naturalist Tradition

Looking Back

Rachel Carson was born into a relatively innocent world that seemed bountiful and full of opportunity. Indeed, Americans had long considered themselves innocent – free from the taint of "old world" corruption – living in a sort of natural paradise made on an Edenic model for their use. Beginning with the first voyagers to the New World, descriptions of America are lush, resplendent, excessive. This is the way most Americans, until fairly recently, have viewed their country: as a cornucopia of natural wonders for their delectation and use.

Nature, though, can be used up. By the time Rachel Carson first began to write, she recognized distinct signs of the abuse of nature. Even as a young woman returning home to the Allegheny Valley after college, she could not but see pollution for what it was. The fishermen in *Under the Sea Wind,* in Carson's mind, showed disregard for the balance that the rest of the natural world intrinsically maintains. When she began to write *Silent Spring,* Carson had witnessed almost two decades of uncontrolled abuse of the natural world by government and industry.

The combination of a child's sense of wonder that never deserted her and an abiding sense of responsibility are at the core of Carson's writing. That twofold focus links Carson to a tradition of American nature writers who saw it as the writer's responsibility to interpret nature for others in order to preserve and protect it. What distinguishes Carson from many earlier writers is her sense of humility. Never in any of her books does she insist on her centrality in the natural world. Unlike many of the nature writers preceding her, Carson never felt that nature was there for her personal use. She is scientist, interested lover of nature, and chronicler of its wonders.

She does not use nature to preach, to make political statements, or to reflect on her own inner reality.

The nature writers preceding Carson were for the most part men whose interests, talents, and vocations as explorers, travelers, scientists, and political activists put them in contact with nature. They brought to their view of nature a sense of their own place in it.

William Bartram

William Bartram, the son of a traveling botanist, was one of the earliest chroniclers of what is now the southeastern United States. Born in Carson's home state in 1723, he saw a Pennsylvania very different from the one Rachel Carson saw in her youth. But even he was looking at a lost world when he accompanied his father, John Bartram, on his trips to Florida to collect and classify flora of the South. America in the eighteenth century was already showing the careless hand of man. A botanist himself, William Bartram also traveled extensively in the South, sending rare specimens of plants from North and South Carolina, Georgia, and Florida to his British botanist friend, John Fothergill. His notes from his travels, published in 1791 and most recently reissued in 1988, describe an American wilderness that was lush and harmonious and soon to disappear. His response to the natural world, a product of poetic vision and careful scrutiny, was one of getting to know the world by naming it, by classifying and cataloging its abundant species. James Dickey says in his introduction to the 1988 edition of *Travels* that "innocence is the main word to use in connection with Bartram's reverential exploration."[1]

Bartram's travels and explorations, full of explosive hyperbole about the landscape, also reveal that civilization is encroaching in every state. While on his journey through the South, he stayed at numerous plantations that were steadily turning the wilderness into agricultural enterprises. Bartram viewed with reverence the wilderness that remained, as this anecdote from his writings shows. While traveling in Georgia, Bartram and his companions camped by a beautiful spring. Several times during the night, the men went back and forth to the spring. In the morning light they noticed a monstrous rattlesnake coiled beside the path. Bartram, upon seeing the snake, was terrified, but he offered "thanksgiving to the supreme Creator and preserver" for his and his companions' lives. He also recognized that "the dignified nature of the generous though terrible creature, who had suffered us all to pass many times by him during the night, without injuring us in the least" (Bartram, 223) was praiseworthy. God and nature, omnipotent and beautiful, are the lodestars of Bartram's life. The snake incident recalled an event from his boyhood when his father pulled him back from a certain encounter with a coiled snake he had not seen. Both incidents offer Bartram the opportunity to extol the beauties of the species. In his adult life, he was able to convince his companions to give the snake its life. The snake from Bartram's youth was not so lucky – the guide killed it and Bartram's father took its skin and fangs.

Throughout his travels, Bartram is aware of the harmony within the natural world that men, such as the guide of his boyhood, disturb, whether for sport, safety, or profit. While he often extemporizes on the ferocity of wilderness creatures, he always returns to wonder at the beauty and the intricate balance of nature. While paddling up a river in Florida searching for rare flora, Bartram witnesses the one-day life of the Ephemera moth. Having deposited their eggs upon the river, the moths swarm together, "gay and tranquil, each meets his beloved mate in the still air, inimitably bedecked in their new nuptial robes. . . . With what peace, love, and joy, do they end the last moments of their existence" (Bartram, 88). He goes on to recount that the entire life cycle of the moth is one year, most of which is spent at the river bottom as a grub. Bartram sees in their existence a lesson for human beings: "The importance of the existence of these beautiful and delicately formed little creatures, whose frame and organization are equally wonderful, more delicate, and perhaps as complicated as those of the most perfect human being, is worth a few moments contemplation. . . . And if we consider the very short period of that stage of existence, which we may reasonably suppose to be the only space of their life that admits of pleasure and enjoyment, what a lesson doth it not afford us of the vanity of our own pursuits" (Bartram, 89).

Ephemeral existence, momentary beauty, ferocious power, horrendous terror – all are a part of the natural world, and all, for Bartram, make his travels in the wilderness journeys into his soul. Nature was for Bartram not only an external reality (perhaps fast diminishing) to be scientifically catalogued but a signpost for the human spirit, for in nature he found the emblems of the spirit, and the closer human beings could get to nature, the closer they got to God and to harmony within themselves.

What brings Bartram to mind in relation to Carson is his capacity for wonder. All of nature received his unabashed response. In his writing, he seems to the twentieth-century reader much like the child in Carson's *A Sense of Wonder.* Bartram, paddling down the rivers of Georgia and Florida, sees the world with the innocent and unjaded eyes of the child. He marvels at everything he sees. Nothing is done for expedience; rather all is done to learn, to appreciate, and to enjoy. It is that legacy that Carson recaptured in her book.

Henry David Thoreau and Ralph Waldo Emerson

Henry David Thoreau, writing almost 60 years after Bartram published his *Travels*, is still considered the guru of American nature writing. He comes to mind not simply because of his enormous stature in the philosophical discussion of the human relationship to the world but also because several of Carson's earlier biographers compared her life unfavorably with his. His solitary existence at Walden Pond is extolled, while her reclusive life, her attempts to find a quiet spot away from the press of the modern world, are viewed as spinsterish and narrow. More important, however, when considering the two writers is to identify their common willingness to confront the world; she in *Silent Spring,* he in *Civil Disobedience* (1849).

Perhaps surprisingly, Carson's *Silent Spring* and Thoreau's *Civil Disobedience* have more in common than do Carson's "nature" writings and *Walden* (1854). In *Silent Spring* and *Civil Disobedience* both naturalists took a public stand that put their other work in jeopardy. Certainly Thoreau's stand was anticipated; he had often taken public positions on the issues of slavery, taxation, war, and public welfare. Carson's publication of the confrontational *Silent Spring* was less to be expected. Their approaches to nature writing, on the other hand, reveal important differences between the two.

That Thoreau saw himself as a voice for nature and for voiceless humanity in his community is evident in *Walden,* as is his sense of his special relationship with the woods: "My purpose in going to Walden Pond was not to live cheaply nor to live dearly there but to transact some private business with the fewest obstacles."[2] The relationship between Thoreau and Walden Pond that flourished in the text always portrays Thoreau as observer/participant in the life of the pond. The focus is on the process of the man more than it is on the processes of nature; even though Thoreau is in nature, it is almost as if he reads it as a book to learn how to live. His observations on time are relevant illustrations on how Thoreau sees himself in the wilderness: "Time is but the stream I go a-fishing in. I drink at it; but while I drink I see the sandy bottom and detect how shallow it is" (*Walden,* 71). This observation puts Thoreau in the center of his world; it is almost a pre-Copernican universe in which he is the focus, the actor, the observer, and the judge of the processes of nature. He is not simply one of the many parts of the natural world.

Further, his observations about the function of nature solidify his place in the world. Again, nature is his book. He asserts: "I did not read books the first summer; I hoed beans" (*Walden,* 79). Indeed, Thoreau's aim in *Walden* is often to describe how much nature can provide for human beings. While he does not think of it in terms of quantitative consumption and urges his readers to "simplify, simplify, simplify," there is, throughout the text a recognition of the ways in which nature serves people and of the ways in which people can learn how to live by studying the processes of nature. In that sense, nature is mediate; it is the tool which teaches people how to live in harmony with themselves and the world around them. Thus those who live in cities and pursue careers often lose touch with the most valuable parts of themselves. It is even possible for those who live close to the earth to lose touch with it and with themselves, for, as Thoreau points out: "I was more independent than any farmer in Concord, for I was not anchored to a house or farm" (*Walden,* 42-43).

Finally, Thoreau's foray into independent living at Walden was prompted by a very focused desire. He said: "I went into the woods because I wished to live deliberately, to front only the essential facts of life, and see if I could not learn what it had to teach, and not, when I came to die, discover that I had not lived" (*Walden,* 66). Indeed, in the school of nature, Thoreau saw himself as a perfect student. He had rejected the trappings of civilization, taken himself out of the round of work, money, and consumption and had gone into the woods to learn the secrets of life from nature, the perfect teacher.

Thoreau, in his sense of nature as mediate, is not very distant from Ralph Waldo Emerson, who, in his essay "Nature" (1836)

speaks of how "Nature stretches out her arms to embrace man," and
when he is in harmony with the natural world, he "makes the central
figure of the visible sphere."[3] Furthermore, Emerson sees nature in
service to human beings, and he emphasizes that role by making it a
sort of handmaiden: "Nature is thoroughly mediate. It is made to
serve. It receives the dominion of man as meekly as the ass on which
the Savior rode" ("Nature," 22). Like Thoreau, Emerson pursues a
relationship with the natural world to glean from it how he and
others should live. It is also in nature that Emerson seeks the divine,
he maintains, "The visible world and the relation of its parts, is the
dial plate of the invisible" ("Nature," 18). Thus, in the study of
nature, Emerson and Thoreau discovered not only how to live but
how to place themselves at the center of the world they observed
and represent for nineteenth-century America a way to find God.

The focus of much nineteenth-century nature writing is on the
responses of the human being to the natural world. Carson, while
clearly a conservationist and an activist on nature's behalf, saw herself, until her last book, as an observer and a translator of natural
facts for the understanding of her audience. She is not, however, at
the center of her books as Thoreau is, aggressively, in his. Nor does
she seek to find, in the realms of the natural world, a spiritual divin-
ity; rather, she is content, like the speaker in Wallace Stevens's
"Sunday Morning," to accept "material immortality."

It is in *Silent Spring* that Carson philosophically approaches
Thoreau's vehemence in *Civil Disobedience.* Her focus in that book
is clearly to change the status quo. Just as Americans in the 1840s
had become trapped by their own expansionist instincts into a war
with Mexico that could not redound to their spiritual benefit, so
Americans in the 1950s had become entrapped by their use of toxic
chemicals that were threatening the natural world and their own
lives. To see the true implications of the Mexican-American War and
to understand the ways in which American values were being distorted were Thoreau's fixed purpose when he refused to pay his poll
taxes and was jailed for a night. The result of that experience found
its way into print in *Civil Disobedience;* the need to question government was given voice and credibility, if not in Thoreau's own
time, then for future generations.

Carson herself in *Silent Spring* refers to the citizen's authority to
question the government. While most Americans give lip service to

the Jeffersonian principle that citizens have the right to declare
themselves free of governments that do not respond to their just
needs, Thoreau saw, in nineteenth-century government, a sort of
bureaucracy that needed to be upset. Over 100 years later, the
bureaucracy, of which Carson was for a good part of her career a
member, was even more complex and immovable. Thus the job of
Silent Spring, to shake the bureaucracy into reexamining its priorities and its responsibilities, was much more difficult. That Carson
was a woman also made her job more difficult, and the response to
her thorough research and careful compilation of data was often to
dismiss her work as the emotional ranting of a hysterical woman. Her
dedication of the book to Albert Schweitzer, who said "Man has lost
the capacity to foresee and forestall. He will end by destroying the
earth," focused the text as a warning and as a prophesy. Her dedication reminded readers, as Thoreau did in *Civil Disobedience*, that
people must take responsibility "for the world in which they live.

Despite the parallels between *Civil Disobedience* and *Silent
Spring*, Thoreau's persistent persona, which is so different from Carson's scientific demeanor, highlights a nineteenth-century attitude
toward nature that even the most insistent nature lover was apt to
fall into. Thoreau used nature as a guide for his own spiritual
growth. Nature constantly pulled Thoreau out of himself and
reminded him of his connection with the rest of the cosmos. He
wrote on 23 August 1852, when he was 35 years old, "I live so much
in my habitual thoughts, a routine of thought, that I forget there is
any outside to the glove, and am surprised when I behold it as
now – yonder hills and river in the moonlight."[4] Thoreau, like
Emerson, Channing, and other Transcendentalists, made the world a
reference for his own spiritual journeys. On 21 August 1851
Thoreau, speculating on the intellectual barrenness of most men,
wrote: "It is the marriage of the soul with Nature that makes the
intellect fruitful, that gives birth to imagination" (*Journals*, 54).

Walking in and around Concord gave Thoreau the opportunity
not simply to observe the landscape as the surveyor he was but to
study his relation to it and to put himself in a larger context. After
one of his many walks, recorded in his journal of 20 June 1850,
Thoreau pointed out that he had a garden larger than any artificial
one planted on a nobleman's grounds (*Journals*, 36). His decision
not to earn a living as a teacher or an office worker left him free to

wander. He recorded: "I can easily walk ten, fifteen, twenty, any number of miles, commencing at my own door, without going by any house, without crossing a road except where the fox and the mink do" (*Journals*, 37). The journals, as well as his larger texts, reveal a man resisting the encroachments of business, commerce, and industry and drawn to nature: "There is a sweet wild world which lies along the strain of the wood thrush – the rich intervales which border the stream of its song – more thoroughly genial to my nature than any other" (*Journals*, 36).

While Carson only later in life had the opportunity to give up her job, she also recognized the lure of wild nature, the wonder that it held for young and old if they would only open themselves to it. Unlike Thoreau, however, she did not see nature chiefly as a vehicle for the spiritual growth of one species. Her focus was often on how nature survives, how the cycles of birth, death, and regeneration in the natural world move apace without any input from the most self-absorbed of species. If nineteenth-century observers like Thoreau and Emerson discovered themselves in nature and reaffirmed their deepest philosophical convictions with emblems from the natural world, Carson, living in a more damaged world, tried to discover the ways in which it survived despite the encroachments of civilization.

John Muir

John Muir, more widely traveled and far more polemical than Thoreau, saw in the Transcendentalist a spiritual progenitor, a man whose approach to nature fostered his own. In his writing, the younger man began where Thoreau, 22 years his elder, left off, and while Thoreau traveled much in Concord, Muir traveled much in search of other natural wonders to discover and extol. Like Thoreau before him, Muir saw in nature a place to understand himself and a place to worship those forces which remained forever beyond human comprehension. Saving that wilderness became his goal in life. Edwin Way Teale said that Muir saw everything in nature as "the handiwork of God. . . . He spoke with the fire of the Covenanters. This religious fervor and spiritual intensity in Muir's response to nature contributed much to the power of his pleading for the cause of conservation." Teale goes on to say, "I know of no other writer, with the exception of Henry Thoreau, who had so pure and lofty a vision of man's ultimate relationship with nature."[5]

The relationship between man and nature was for Muir central to his existence. An iconoclast like Thoreau, he had little regard for the opinion of others, and he gave up several lucrative careers to pursue his study of nature. Again like Thoreau, he felt himself rich because he had all he wanted, not because he had a lot. An ardent individualist, Muir is reminiscent of the Concord philosopher especially in the forthright way he expresses his opinions without regard for social conventions. "I was fond of everything that was wild," Muir says in an autobiographical sketch, "and all my life I've been growing fonder and fonder of wild places and wild creatures" (*Wilderness*, 3).

That love of wildness focused much of his writing about the natural world. In his 23 March 1856 journal entry, Thoreau decries the loss of the wilderness around Concord: "I spend a considerable portion of my time observing the habits of the wild animals, my brute neighbors. By their various movement and migrations they fetch the year about to me. . . . But when I consider that the nobler animals have been exterminated here – the cougar, panther, lynx, wolverine, wolf, bear, moose, deer, the beaver, the turkey, etc., etc., – I cannot but feel as if I lived in a tamed, and, as it were, emasculated country" (*Journals*, 157). The loss of wildness, already effected on the Eastern coast, is what Muir sought to prevent in the wilderness of Yosemite and Alaska.

Born in Dunbar, Scotland, on 21 April 1838, Muir spent his childhood in confrontation with his domineering and religiously fanatic father. In 1849 his father broke with his church and brought his family to America, where he bought a farm in southeastern Wisconsin. When Muir was 22 and yearning to be on his own, a neighbor suggested he take some of the inventions he had been working on to the state fair in Madison. From there Muir tried university life, but, unlike Thoreau, he was ill prepared for it. He attended college off and on until Civil War conscription threatened him, and he headed north to Canada. While there he lived for months in the woods studying the flora of the region. It was in the swampy forests above Lake Huron that Muir experienced an epiphany that he ranked with his later meeting with Emerson.[6]

He saw two Calypso Borealis white flowers standing alone in the swamp. Those flowers, Muir realized, were only by chance seen by a human being; they did not serve a special function or have a particular use. That moment set Muir to thinking about the function of nature. He asked, "Are not all plants beautiful? or in some way useful? Would not the world suffer by the banishment of a single weed?" (Fox, 44). The focus of the naturalist begins to shift. Nature does not need man to justify itself, even though human beings often need nature to understand themselves. His epiphany, along with his reading of Darwin, shifted his focus from human beings to nature, whose beauty and wildness did not need explanation or justification. The ideal of God he had fought about with his sternly Calvinistic father was transformed, by his study of nature and his growing sense of the totality and necessity of all parts of the world, into a conviction that focused the rest of his life. He concluded that "the universe would be incomplete without man, but it would also be incomplete without the smallest transmicroscopic creature that dwells beyond our conceitful eyes and knowledge" (Fox, 53).

In the process of coming to terms with his relationship to the wilderness, he also concluded that Emerson and Thoreau, the two lights in his philosophical life, were, as Stephen Fox points out, "insufficiently wild" (Fox, 83). He felt that Thoreau and Emerson went to nature with a philosophical schema, whereas he wanted to find that schema in nature. He would certainly have agreed with Thoreau that Concord was "emasculated country," but he felt that Thoreau should have traveled farther, not so much in Concord.

Muir also began to see the connection between the natural world and the economic policies of the burgeoning capitalist economy. "Natural wonders," he felt, "could not be protected within the assumptions of radically individualist capitalism" (Fox, 86). If America were going to preserve the wilderness areas still remaining in the 1880s, the time had come to stand firm on behalf, Muir believed.

In the 1890s, as when Carson was writing *Silent Spring* in the 1950s, there were those whose goal it was to protect the natural world and those whose aim it was to harm the natural world as effectively as possible for public convenience and for profit. Muir first attacked the issue of wilderness preservation in his fight to save Yosemite. As was later the case when Carson began digging into the relationship between big business and government in her research for *Silent Spring,* of the various interest groups involved in the struggle over Yosemite, it seemed that everybody had a voice except nature itself. No one was protecting its interests. But the struggle to save Yosemite also produced a way of approaching the politics of conservation that has remained in place for a century.

In 1889 John Muir and the editor of *Century* magazine, Robert Underwood Johnson, who had worked unceasingly with Muir to create a wilderness preserve in the Sierra Nevada mountains, began to think about ways to counterbalance the enormous power of government and big business. To preserve California's natural wonders they formed the Sierra Club, modeling it after the Appalachian Mountain Club. Muir, despite his misgivings about his organizational skills, was elected its first president (Fox, 106-7), a post he held until his death in 1914. In the years following the club's inception, Muir focused his attention on keeping Yosemite "forever wild" (Fox, 111). It was not an easy task; logging and mining interests were constantly challenging the U.S. Senate to open up the forest reserves for commercial use.

Ironically, Muir and Carson had to deal with the same government agency in their campaigns. The Department of Agriculture, which was Carson's nemesis throughout the controversy surrounding *Silent Spring*, also had a hand in what Muir considered the greatest crime against nature – the felling of ancient forests. Muir and Carson both came up against policy that, on the surface, implied "the greatest good for the greatest number in the long run" (Fox, 111). Just as Muir constantly had to defend his position on unmanaged wilderness because he could not quantify its value for the forest service, so Carson was constantly defending the lives of birds against the farmer's crop or the suburbanite's garden.

Another analogy between Muir's and Carson's crusades is that both conservationists were writing at the end of an era. The 1890 census proclaimed the end of the frontier (Fox, 115), so Muir was in the position to create policy for the next era in American history. Carson, too, wrote at the end on an era, World War II. With the development of the atomic bomb and the production of chemical pesticides, Carson saw the end of a world in which human beings could with any conscience continue using nature for their own ends without considering the consequences. *Silent Spring* was her policy statement on how we should proceed.

Like Carson after him, Muir saw the harmony in nature. He did not want to save the trees to the exclusion of other aspects of nature; rather, he saw the trees as part of an intricately designed whole that depended upon all of its parts. Like Carson, he too saw the world in terms of physical laws in which human beings had only a small part. Stephen Fox calls Muir an "intuitive ecologist" (Fox, 291), but however he is designated, his sense of the world is central to the late nineteenth- and early twentieth-century conservation movement; it is this movement that Carson herself was very much in tune with. Wildness is necessary to maintain the balance between human beings and the rest of nature, and both Muir and Carson saw the consequences of upsetting that balance.

Aldo Leopold

Another intuitive ecologist, Aldo Leopold, also saw the harmony in nature and framed it in much the same way that Carson did in her earliest article on the sea. Carson summarized "Undersea" in its concluding paragraph, saying, "Thus we see the parts fall into place: The water receiving from earth and air the simple materials, storing them up until the gathering energy of the spring sun wakens the sleeping plants to a burst of dynamic activity, hungry swarms of planktonic animals growing and multiplying upon the abundant plants, and themselves falling prey to the shoals of fish; all, in the end, to be redissolved into their component substances when the inexorable laws of the sea demand it" ("Undersea," 29). The interconnectedness and interdependence of all life is clearly stated in Carson's earliest published work and repeated throughout her writing. The timelessness of nature, its endurance, and its watchful presence are somehow beyond human grasp unless human beings are willing to return to nature with reverence and wonder. It is only then that they can comprehend what might be the basis of any religion Carson might have professed: "material immortality."

The continuity and endurance of nature far beyond the span of human life and memory is a theme that emerges from many of the earlier nature writers, and Aldo Leopold senses that continuity in *A Sand County Almanac* (1949). In his essays on conservation, Leopold highlights the continuance of nature on land as Carson does for the sea. In a short sketch entitled "Odyssey," Leopold follows an atom locked in the rock in Sand County in its "material immortality" and its incarnations until it is carried back to the sea and another atom in the rock begins its timeless migration. As in Carson's picture of the sea, there is continuity but very little sense of time. There is no rush. First the atom emerges from the limestone ledge as a part of a burr oak, which "fattened a deer, which fed an Indian, all in a single year."[7] With the death of the Indian, the atom is quiescent for a time, then reemerges in the bluestem leaf to protect the plover's eggs. Underground again, it "lay in the soil, foot-loose and fancy-free" (Leopold, 112). But the cycle continues on land, much as it is described as happening in the sea: "Next he [the atom] entered a tuft of side-oats grama, a buffalo, a buffalo chip, and again the soil. Next a spiderwort, a rabbit, and an owl, thence a tuft of sporobolus" (Leopold, 112). This cyclical reincarnation of the atom continues until finally it is back in the sea, but "for every atom lost to the sea, the prairie pulls another out of the decaying rocks" (Leopold, 114), and thus the cycle is endless. Like Carson, Leopold respected that cycle and tried, in his relationship with his farm, to respect it. He valued the land that most farmers rejected, the plants that struggled to live in the rigorous environment of his landscape, and he recognized the part each played in the cycles of the seasons.

Perhaps the most compelling metaphor for the endurance and regeneration of the natural world is paradoxically portrayed in the cutting down of a large oak on Leopold's farm. The oak contains in its rings the history of the county. Having sprouted in 1865, at the end of the Civil War, the oak represents for Leopold a "collective immortality," much like Carson's "material immortality." He sees in its rings "the perpetual battle within and among species" (Leopold, 7), and in cutting it down for firewood Leopold remembers the history of his county and recognizes his part in the cycles of nature. As he burns his oak to heat his kettle and warm his home, he promises, "Those ashes, come spring, I will return to the orchard at the foot of the sandhill. They will come back to me again, perhaps as red apples, or perhaps as a spirit of enterprise in some fat October squirrel, who, for reasons unknown to himself, is bent on planting acorns" (Leopold, 19).

Like Thoreau and Muir before him, Leopold recognized how human beings became enmeshed in the processes of nature, and he argues for added responsibility with added control. It is the power that human beings gain over nature through their use of tools that adds to their burden to conserve the world, and Leopold's definition of a conservationist emphasizes that knowledge and power do not imply divine rule: "A conservationist is one who is humbly aware that

with each stroke he is writing his signature on the face of his land"
(Leopold, 73). Indeed, while tending his land, Leopold comes to
know that "the Lord giveth, and the Lord taketh away, but He is no
longer the only one to do so. When some remote ancestor of ours
invented the shovel, he became a giver: he could plant a tree. And
when the axe was invented, he became a taker: he could chop it
down. Whoever owns land has thus assumed, whether he knows it
or not, the divine functions of creating and destroying plants"
(Leopold, 72). Power and humility, those are the complementary
elements in Leopold's world. Human beings have power, but they
must use it with humility.

On his isolated farm, Leopold felt much like Thoreau did in his
woods at Walden. Both men learned from and came to very similar
conclusions about the world around them. Leopold learned that
"every farm woodland, in addition to yielding lumber, fuel, and
posts, should provide its owner a liberal education. This crop of
wisdom never fails, but it is not always harvested" (Leopold, 78-9).
Like Thoreau, Leopold kept a journal of his education, and in *Sand
County Almanac* he noted, "I here record some of the many lessons
I have learned in my own woods" (Leopold, 79).

Henry Beston

The tradition of nature writing carries with it an obligation to speak
for the natural world. Bartram, Thoreau, Muir, Leopold – all sought
in nature the harmony they missed in communion with society. The
lessons of nature formed the core of their spiritual lives and those
lessons, passed on in their nature writings, are central to much of
Carson's work as well; Henry Beston's *The Outermost House*, however, was the book that influenced her most deeply. Like Thoreau,
who also went to Cape Cod to get to know the ocean, Beston built
himself an isolated cottage on the dunes near Eastham Life Saving
Station. He intended the house as a vacation retreat, but in the fall of
1926 he went to spend a year there, living like Thoreau, alone with
his journals and with the cycles of the season. *The Outermost House*
is a result of his solitude and journal writing during that year.

Perhaps Beston's house and his book held such an attraction for
her because Carson always longed for the ocean. She might also
have regarded the book so highly because of Beston's consummate
skill as a writer, who spent hours at his craft. Like Carson, Beston

was a poet of nature, and in his poetry Carson found much that spoke to her own vision of the ocean. In *The Edge of the Sea,* Carson herself focused on some of the parts of the ocean's system that Beston had introduced in *The Outermost House.* Although his book is not specifically focused on tides and the flora and fauna of the tidal region, as is Carson's, Beston is aware of what the sea takes and gives to the land through the tides. He often wanders away from the sea, inland into the marshland, discourses on the birds of the region, and laments the fact that "our fantastic civilization has fallen out of touch with many aspects of nature."[8] His year on Cape Cod is an attempt, like Thoreau's in *Walden,* to come to terms with the meaning of his life and with his relationship to nature and to civilization.

Like Carson, he too was taken with the habits of birds, and he catalogs many of them as they come and go on the cape. But perhaps his most significant image is that of the young swimmer. The picture, drawn at the close of the book, sums up Beston's idyllic relationship with the natural world. It is late August. Soon Beston will leave the cape. As he is walking on the dunes, he sees a naked swimmer hurling himself headlong into the waves and returning to the land. Beston comments: "It was all a beautiful thing to see: the surf thundering across the great natural world, the beautiful and compact body in its naked strength and symmetry, the astounding plunge across the air" (Beston, 215-16). All is harmony. This is the ideal relationship between man and the world. Human beings, like nature, have beauty and harmony, but so often they lose it in their struggle to live in the "stench modern civilization breathes" (Beston, 189). Beston retreats to the beach where he can "dwell in a world that has good natural smell, that is full of keen, vivid, and interesting savours and fragrances" (Beston, 191).

Looking Forward

The cycles of the seasons, the interdependence of all elements of the natural world, the sense of endurance, continuity, and immortality – all intermingle in Beston, as they do in Bartram, Thoreau, Muir, and Leopold, and finally reach a poetic crescendo in Rachel Carson. Her books about the sea incorporate the world vision of many earlier writer-naturalists. They belong in and expand and enrich the tradition of American nature writing. *Silent Spring* also looks back longingly on that world. There is in the book a hope that the harmony can be restored, that human beings can find a way to life in nature without destroying it, and that people can learn from nature's cycles ways to live in harmony with the world. *Silent Spring* does not simply look back and long to recapture paradise, however. It looks aggressively forward to a new type of nature writing.

While there was an increasing awareness among nineteenth- and early twentieth-century nature writers that nature had to be preserved, the political action writers of the late twentieth century present an almost united front in condemning human behavior in regard to the environment. Compared with later writers, Carson's warnings in *Silent Spring* seem positively moderate. Her central concern was the preservation of the earth and human beings, despite their attempts to destroy themselves along with all other species. That concern became, in the 1970s and 1980s, a battle cry for political ecologists.

There are three books that owe their existence, in large part, to what Carson was able to achieve with *Silent Spring*. Each has a different sphere of influence, but they arise from the same concern that fostered Carson's book. In 1982 Jonathan Schell published *The Fate of the Earth*, which was first released, like *Silent Spring*, serially in *New Yorker*. It created for the first time a coherent picture of what would happen to the world in the event of a major nuclear war. In 1989 Bill McKibben published *The End of Nature* and John McPhee published *The Control of Nature*, which track to their logical conclusions the philosophies that human beings have an intrinsic right to control and alter the patterns of nature. While there might be less danger of nuclear war today with the dissolution of the Soviet Union and the concerted effort on the part of major powers to disarm nuclear warheads and to control their proliferation, there is still the very real danger of nuclear accidents, as Three Mile Island and Chernobyl sadly illustrate. Any major accident could radically change the ecosystem. There is also the continued and persistent danger to the world because of what people do to it in the name of progress, commerce, and profit. The loss of the rain forests is only one example of what damage to one part of the ecosystem can do to all parts.

All three books focus, as did Carson in *Silent Spring*, on the wisdom of the need to control the environment to achieve maximum comfort for certain people or to gain political power for one group over another. Thus with *Silent Spring* begins a new era, the era of political ecology. While Muir and the Sierra Club took a real stand on behalf of voiceless nature with state and federal agencies, and the Appalachian Mountain Club sought to protect certain wilderness retreats and trails, neither group actually anticipated what Carson did in *Silent Spring*. It was not until the 1970s and 1980s that the need for a political lobby to save the earth became apparent.

Jonathan Schell

In 1982, Jonathan Schell was faced with a problem similar to Carson's when she was writing *Silent Spring*. She had concrete evidence of the devastation that pesticides were already causing; Schell had the horrific examples of Hiroshima and Nagasaki. But both were, in effect, working in an area that had no real past history to confirm or deny their assertions. Both could only project into a future they hoped their books would help prevent. Both feared the lack of control over technologies with a tremendous capacity for long-term destruction. Schell saw that "while science is without doubt the most powerful revolutionary force in our world, no one directs that force."[9]

Within the 20 years between the publication of *Silent Spring* and the publication of *The Fate of the Earth*, it also became far more obvious to nonscientific readers that "we are ignorant about where we fit in, and most of all about the enormous, imponderable system of life in which we are embedded as working parts. We really do not understand nature at all" (Schell, 73). Carson's work had forced readers to think about how little they understood the ecosystem, and the possibility of nuclear holocaust reinforced people's anxieties about the impact on the environment of forces they could neither fully understand nor control. In fact, Schell, in the tradition of Carson, saw what he referred to as the "strong reciprocal influences" of all parts of nature. So while Carson pointed out how pesticides, in damaging one part of the system, could have a deleterious impact on the whole ecosystem, Schell saw the impact in terms of ozone reduction (also related to the problem of global warming, so cogently described by Bill McKibben). He points out that

> the parts of this delicately balanced whole include, among many others, the chemical composition of both the troposphere and the stratosphere;

the temperature levels of the atmosphere and the degree of moisture at all
altitudes; the temperature and reflectivity of the earth's surface; the circulatory patterns of the air; the circulatory patterns of the ocean currents;
and the degree of retention of the earth's reflected warmth by the atmosphere, in the so-called greenhouse effect. Each of these parts could be
disturbed by a holocaust, and the disturbance of any one could disturb
many or all the others (Schell, 88-89)

No one part is free from the influence of any other part, nor would
any part escape a major cataclysm, such as nuclear war.

The control of the world that people thought they had gained
with the splitting of the atom and the discovery of the "secrets of
nature" really creates an enormous burden, for now they are
responsible for the world which they have created. In her speech to
the graduates at Scripps College in June 1962, Carson foreshadowed
Schell's concern. She pointed out that when Francis Thompson said
in the 1800s, "Thou canst not stir a flower / without troubling a
star," he realized poetically what humans had not yet accepted
scientifically. In fact, she continued, "Man's attitude toward nature is
today critically important simply because of his new-found power to
destroy it."[10] She went on to speak specifically about the issue of
radiation: "I clearly remember that in the days before Hiroshima I
used to wonder whether nature – nature in the broadest context of
the word – actually needed protection from man. Surely the sea was
inviolate and forever beyond man's power to change it. . . . But I was
wrong. Even these things, that seemed to belong to the eternal veri-
ties, are not only threatened but have already felt the destroying
hand of man" (Scripps).

Bill McKibben

Bill McKibben, as well as John McPhee, sees nature at the point to
which Carson hoped it would never come. That point is the title of
McKibben's book, *The End of Nature.* Carson wanted to curtail the
destructive forces that could destroy the environment, such as
chemical and radioactive pollution, but what happened in the years
after her death is a kind of accretion. Despite controls and standards,
pollution has simply increased incrementally to the point that we are
now, according to McKibben, witnessing the end of nature
as we know it. Ironically, it isn't because of radioactive fallout or

because of chemical poisoning, although neither he nor other environmentalists dismiss these concerns. Rather, the culprit is carbon dioxide, the compound we expel into the air with each breath and spew out of cars and factories. The major problem, as McKibben sees it, is that "we have increased the amount of carbon dioxide in the air by about 25 percent in the last century, and will almost certainly double it in the next; and we have added a soup of other gases. *We have substantially altered the earth's atmosphere*" (McKibben's italics).[11]

With this remark we have actually reached the point Carson referred to in her Scripps College speech. She felt that her generation had "brought into being a fatal and destructive power" (Scripps), and she was not sanguine about the possibilities for the future. That future might not have taken precisely the path Carson feared, but the result is as significant. McKibben sees that change not just in physical but in metaphysical terms. He points out that "the end of nature is not an impersonal event, like an earthquake. It is something we humans have brought about through a series of conscious and unconscious choices: *we* ended the natural atmosphere, and hence the natural climate, and hence the natural boundaries of the forests, and so on. In so doing, we exhibit a kind of power thought in the past to be divine" (McKibben, 78)

McKibben's assessment of human behavior brings up another point for which Carson's work opened the way. Since the sixteenth century and the rise of modern science, scientific process has been seen as inviolate. Scientists discover the secrets of nature and harness them for human good. The scientist was not seen as responsible for what he discovered. Knowledge per se was the end of science, and in that respect, scientific research was privileged. What Carson did in *Silent Spring* was to highlight the necessity for scientists to take responsibility for the things they discovered. Having the capability to create chemicals that could destroy the natural environment is not equivalent with having the right to use those chemicals. Coming as it did at approximately the same time as the work on the atomic bomb, work on DDT was seen as a way of gaining control over the natural environment, just as the threat of the atomic bomb could control the political environment. It is a tribute to Carson's plea in *Silent Spring* and her continued efforts after the book's publication that attitudes about the natural environment began to change in the late 1960s. Resistance to the use of napalm and Agent Orange in Vietnam, resistance to uncontrolled and unregulated dumping of sewage, resistance to the spewing out of factory wastes and uncontrolled car emissions herald a change in the layperson's attitude toward the environment.

McKibben traces much of the historical problem of damage to the environment to the intense human desire to control it. What McKibben recognizes, and what ecologists such as Bill Devall and George Sessions advocate in *Deep Ecology* (1985), is the need to ask "more searching questions about human life, society and nature."[12] Those questions, which Devall and Sessions say are exemplified in the work of Aldo Leopold and Rachel Carson, focus on why human beings need to see themselves as "separate and superior to the rest of Nature" (Devall and Sessions, 65).

Devall and Sessions, like McKibben, see that view as part of larger Western cultural patterns, which have "become increasingly obsessed with the idea of *dominance:* with dominance of human over nonhuman Nature, masculine over the feminine, wealthy and powerful over the poor, with the dominance of the West over non-Western cultures. Deep ecological consciousness allows us to see through these erroneous and dangerous illusions" (Devall and Sessions, 66). The principles of so-called deep ecology, formulated by Devall and Sessions, became the core of McKibben's view for saving the world. They are: "1. Everything is connected to everything else. 2. Everything must go somewhere. 3. Nature knows best. 4. There is no such thing as a free lunch" (Devall and Sessions, 87).

These principles could easily be said to be the very ones that Carson espoused in her attempts to get government to rethink environmental policy in the early 1960s. Then as now, McKibben points out, these principles are more easily articulated than enacted: "the difficulty is certainly more psychological than intellectual – less that we can't figure out major alterations in our way of life than that we simply don't want to. Even if our way of life has destroyed nature and endangered the planet, it is so hard to imagine living in any other fashion" (McKibben, 192).

John McPhee

Specific examples of the conquest of nature are the subject of John McPhee's *The Control of Nature*, in which the author shows how human beings, in their need to dominate and determine all aspects of their environment, often ignore nature's more encompassing plan. McPhee points out that we pit human comfort and security against the natural world rather than keeping the two in harmony: "We are fighting Mother Nature. . . . It's a battle we have to fight day by day, year by year; the health of our economy depends on victory."[13] The quotation refers to the Army Corps of Engineers' battle against the Mississippi River, which over the thousands of years had shaped Louisiana by changing course and building up new land. Had it not done so, Louisiana would simply have been a narrow spit sticking out into the Gulf of Mexico.

The processes of the Mississippi were natural ones that, over time, built up rich wetlands, bayous, and swamps. McPhee points out that "for the Mississippi to make such a change was completely natural, but in the interval since the last shift Europeans had settled beside the river, a nation had developed, and the nation could not afford nature" (McPhee, 6). Nature, McPhee goes on to say, "in this place, had become an enemy of the state" (McPhee, 7). As a geologist who works for the Army Corps of Engineers at the New Orleans district told McPhee, "The Mississippi wants to go West" (McPhee, 54). Eventually, no controls, no floodgates, no levees, no Army Corps of Engineers is going to be able to stop it.

Meanwhile, New Orleans will sink farther and farther below sea level; every tropical storm will threaten floods, and every hurricane may be the one that could change the Mississippi's course. In the meantime, the corps will struggle to keep up the pumping stations, to maintain the levees, and to pump out New Orleans after every storm. But as the *Washington Post* commented in a November 1980 editorial: "Who will win as this slow-motion confrontation between humankind and nature goes on? No one really knows. But after watching Mt. St. Helens and listening to the guesses about its performance, if we had to bet, we would bet on the river" (McPhee, 50).

In another essay in *The Control of Nature,* McPhee chronicles the story of "Los Angeles against the Mountains." It is another story of nature wanting to do one thing and human beings wanting to do something else. The Los Angeles basin is a perfect stage for a conflict with nature, and McPhee sees in that conflict, as he saw in the conflict with the Mississippi River, a paradigm for what is happening in the late twentieth century. Nature will continue to seek ways to survive, and human beings will continue to seek ways to tame it, to keep it in check, so that life as they want it can go on. Of Los Angeles, McPhee says, "A metropolis that exists in a semidesert, imports water three hundred miles, has inveterate flash floods, is at the grinding edges of two tectonic plates, and has a microclimate tenacious of noxious oxides will have its priorities among the aspects of its environment that it attempts to control" (McPhee, 191).

Los Angeles has to be ever alert for debris flows from the San Gabriel Mountains. Like New Orleans, it is a city under siege. As New Orleans has built levees, pumping stations, and spillway diversions, so Los Angeles has built debris basins and numerous cribs to contain the debris flows that come inexorably down the mountain: "Strung out along the San Gabriel front are at least a hundred and twenty bowl-shaped excavations that resemble football stadiums and are often as large" (McPhee, 192). They are intended to catch and contain debris as it flows down the mountain, much like lava. Added to these basins are series of cribs that are meant "to convert plunging streams into boulder staircases, and hypothetically cause erosion to work against itself" (McPhee, 193). McPhee points out that Los Angeles has been very successful in controlling nature: "Against the prodigious odds, Los Angeles is much more successful than it may appear to be. . . . To date, the debris basins have trapped twenty million tons of mountain" (McPhee, 266).

The language of war Carson used in *Silent Spring* and her philosophy of working with nature rather than against it are both evident in McPhee's work.

Ecofeminism

Rachel Carson did not call herself a feminist, but her ideas about the connectedness of the natural world and her sense that a violation of one part of it influences the whole has been embraced by ecofeminists. Ynestra King defined *ecofeminism* as being "about connectedness and wholeness of theory and practice. It asserts the special strength and integrity of every living thing. For us [ecofeminists], the snail darter is to be considered side by side with a community's need for water, the porpoise side by side with appetite for tuna."[14] Ecofeminists perceive the violation of nature as being predicated on the same belief in dominance as the rape of women. Its aim is to redress political, social, and personal structures to achieve connection and wholeness and to nullify dominance.

Ecofeminism argues that the oppression of nature, like the oppression of women, is systematic and a product of patriarchy. H. Patricia Hynes, who has done a thorough feminist analysis of *Silent Spring*, points out that "the atomic bomb was the mid-century touchstone of male dominance" (Hynes, 181). What Carson and other concerned scientists urged in the 1960s was a reevaluation of pesticide use in an ethical framework. In fact, Carson herself pointed out that simply because we have the technology, we do not have an inalienable right to use it. While Carson did not specifically target women as the victims of technology, she was deeply concerned with the reproductive implications of the uncontrolled use of pesticides.

Another ecofeminist, Rachel L. Bagby, further elucidates the philosophy of ecofeminism, saying that it names patriarchy, with its cultural ethics of separation, control, dominance, hierarchical structure, and suppression of emotions and other unquantifiable aspects of being, as the root cause of contemporary ecological and social problems. "The domination of nature is rooted in the domination of person over person, male over female, me over not-me," she writes. "As an alternative . . . ecofeminism advocates participatory modes of interacting. It is inclusive – mind, body, spirit, and emotions, inner and outer development, individual and social responsibility."[15]

At the heart of *Silent Spring* is the notion that "the history of life on earth has been a history of interaction between living things and their surroundings. . . . Only within the moment of time represented by the present century has one species – man – acquired significant power to alter the nature of his world" (Scripps). It is in the twentieth century that man has achieved the dominance he has been struggling for since Francis Bacon, the "father of modern science," linked the control of disorderly nature with the control of women.[16]

Conclusion

Interconnectedness and wholeness, a sense of the integrity of every living thing, the center of the ecofeminist movement, is also the center of *Silent Spring*. But this philosophy is not expressed only in her last book. Her earliest piece for the *Atlantic* revealed her sense that most people did not respect that integrity. She saw the imbalance that "man, the predator," created with the vast harvest he took yearly from the sea. Yet she recognized that it was almost impossible for the human mind to visualize conditions in the "uttermost depths of the ocean." Carson's picture of ocean life was her first statement of the web of connectedness: "Every living thing of the ocean, plant and animal alike, returns to the water at the end of its own life span the materials that had been temporarily assembled to form its body. So there descends into the depths a gentle never-ending rain of the disintegrating particles of what once were living creatures of the sunlit surface waters, or of those twilight regions beneath" ("Undersea," 26). For Carson, the connection was not just causal, it was temporal; the past lived for her in the present: "Individual elements are lost to view, only to reappear again and again in different incarnations" ("Undersea," 29).

Perhaps it is Carson's willingness to accept nature's incomprehensible work that left her open to the challenge and the insinuations of the chemical companies when she published *Silent Spring*. A person who accepted the possibility of mystery could not be a "scientist." Admitting there were some things in nature we could not know, could not control, limited man's dominion. Thus Carson, because she cautioned humility in the face of nature, was considered unscientific. Humility is also a feminine virtue, not one likely to be valued by the conglomerate of chemical companies arrayed against Carson.

While Hynes and other Carson biographers set *Silent Spring* apart from her other books, the books are all connected. The balanced scientific insight and beauty of Carson's *Silent Spring* would not have been possible without the previous books. It is the sense of wonder about nature and the web of life that ties all the books together and that makes *Silent Spring* more than a polemic and more than a scientific treatise. Carson said early in her work on the book that the problem was not simply to make her readers aware of pesticides and their destruction but to make everyone see his or her connection to the problem. In a letter to Carson on 7 February 1958, E. B. White wrote: "I think the whole vast subject of pollution . . . is of the utmost interest and concern to everybody. It starts in the kitchen and extends to Jupiter and Mars. Always some special group or interest is represented, never the earth itself" (Brooks, 237). No one has represented the interests of the earth more faithfully or better taught its value than Rachel Carson: "The earth's vegetation is a part of a web of life in which there are intimate and essential relations between plants and the earth, between plants and other plants, between plants and animals, and we must learn to respect that fine and fragile web if there is to be anything left for the next generation" (*SS*, 64).

Notes and References

Chapter One

1. Philip Sterling, *Sea and Earth: The Life of Rachel Carson* (New York: Thomas Y. Crowell Company, 1970), 30; hereafter cited in text.

2. H. Patricia Hynes, *The Recurring Silent Spring* (New York: Pergamon Press, 1989), 65; hereafter cited in text.

3. "Broken Lamps," as well as most of Carson's other unpublished writings, including college papers, correspondence, research files, and notes for her four books are housed in the Rachel Carson Collection, Beinecke Rare Book and Manuscript Library, Yale University. Permission to quote from the collection received from Beinecke Library and Frances Collins Literary Agency, Trustee of the Rachel Carson Papers; documents in the collection referred to in the text hereafter cited in text as Beinecke papers.

4. Dorothy Thompson Seif, "How I Remember Rachel," *Recorder: The Chatham Alumnae Magazine* 54, no. 2 (Spring 1985): 9.

5. Paul Brooks, *The House of Life: Rachel Carson at Work* (1972; reprint, Boston: Houghton Mifflin, 1989), 19; hereafter cited in text.

6. Dorothy Thompson Seif, "Letters from Rachel Carson: A Young Scientist Sets Her Cause," unpublished manuscript, copyright 1987; paraphrased courtesy of the Rachel Carson Council.

7. Margaret Rossiter, *Women Scientists in America* (Baltimore: Johns Hopkins University Press, 1982); hereafter cited in text.

8. Robert Fulford, "When Jane Jacobs Took on the World," *New York Times Book Review*, 16 February 1992, 28.

9. "The Bat Knew It First," *Colliers*, 18 November 1944, 24.

10. Bob Hines, "Remembering Rachel," *Yankee Magazine*, June 1991, 62; hereafter cited in text.

Chapter Two

1. "Undersea," *Atlantic Monthly*, September 1937; reprint, Brooks, *The House of Life*, 22. All quotations are from the Brooks reprint; hereafter cited in text as "Undersea."

2. Foreword to *Under the Sea Wind* (New York: Simon and Schuster, 1941), xii; hereafter cited in text as foreword, *USW* 1941.

3. *Under the Sea Wind* (New York: Dutton, 1991), 3; hereafter cited in text as *USW*.

4. Carson's notebooks for her four books, which are held in the Beinecke Library, are neither dated nor numbered.

5. Frieda Fordham, *An Introduction to Jung's Psychology* (Baltimore: Penguin Books, 1973), 21.

6. Review of *Under the Sea Wind, New York Times*, 23 November 1941. In Beinecke papers.

7. Review of *Under the Sea Wind, Baltimore Sun*, 2 November 1941. In Beinecke papers.

8. Interview with Shirley Briggs, 9 July 1991; hereafter cited in text.

9. Interview with Shirley Briggs, 10 July 1991.

10. *Chincoteague: A National Wildlife Refuge*, Conservation in Action, no. 1 (Washington, D.C.: Government Printing Office, 1947), 1; hereafter cited in text as *Chincoteague*.

11. Letter to Shirley Briggs from Katherine Howe, 25 September 1946, courtesy of the Rachel Carson Council.

12. *Parker River: A National Wildlife Refuge*, Conservation in Action, no. 2 (Washington, D.C.: Government Printing Office, 1947), 1; hereafter cited in text as *Parker River*.

13. *Mattamuskeet: A National Wildlife Refuge*, Conservation in Action, no. 4 (Washington, D.C.: Government Printing Office, 1947), 4; hereafter cited in text as *Mattamuskeet*.

14. *Bear River: A National Wildlife Refuge*, Conservation in Action, no. 8 (Washington, D.C.: Government Printing Office, 1950), 3; hereafter cited in text as *Bear River*.

15. *Guarding Our Wildlife Resources*, Conservation in Action, no. 5 (Washington, D.C.: Government Printing Office, 1948).

Chapter Three

1. *The Sea around Us*, rev. ed. (New York: Oxford University Press, 1961), 8.

2. Elizabeth Anticaglia, "Rachel Carson," *Twelve American Women* (Chicago: Nelson Hall, 1975), 8.

3. Acceptance speech, American Association of University Women Achievement Award, 22 June 1956, quoted in Brooks, *The House of Life*, 151.

4. *The Edge of the Sea* (1955; reprint, Boston: Houghton Mifflin, 1983), 1; hereafter cited in text as *ES*.

5. Carol Gartner, *Rachel Carson* (New York: Frederick Ungar, 1983), 76; hereafter cited in text.

6. Review of *The Edge of the Sea, U.S. Quarterly Book Review* 12, no. 1 (March 1956). In Beinecke papers.

7. *Washington Star Pictorial Magazine*, 8 March 1953. In Beinecke papers.

8. *A Sense of Wonder* (New York: Harper and Row, 1965), 55.

Chapter Four

1. Robert B. Downs, "Upsetting the Balance of Nature," *Books That Changed America* (London: Macmillian Co., 1970), 260; hereafter cited in text.

2. James Whorton, *Before Silent Spring* (Princeton, N.J.: Princeton University Press, 1974), 248-29; hereafter cited in text.

3. *Silent Spring* (Boston: Houghton Mifflin, 1962), 35; hereafter cited in text as *SS*.

4. Frank Graham, Jr., *Since Silent Spring* (Boston: Houghton Mifflin, 1970), 111; hereafter cited in text.

5. U.S. Department of Health, Education, and Welfare, Office of the Secretary, Washington, D.C., 14 November 1959.

6. See supplement 209 of the *Public Health Report* (Washington, D.C.: Government Printing Office, 1948).

7. W. C. Hueper, *Newer Developments in Occupational and Environmental Cancers,* American Medical Association pamphlet. In Beinecke papers.

8. "The *Silent Spring* of Rachel Carson," on "CBS Reports," 3 April 1963; rebroadcast on PBS 24 July 1981; hereafter cited in text as "CBS Reports." Typescript in Beinecke papers.

Chapter Five

1. William Bartram, *Travels*, introduction by James Dickey (New York: Penguin Books, 1988), ix; hereafter cited in text.

2. Henry David Thoreau, *Walden* (New York: New American Library, 1960), 18; hereafter cited in text as *Walden*.

3. Ralph Waldo Emerson, "Nature," in *The Selected Writings of Ralph Waldo Emerson,* ed. Brooks Atkinson (New York: Modern Library, 1950), 12; hereafter cited in text as "Nature."

4. Odell Shepard, ed., *The Heart of Thoreau's Journals* (New York: Dover Publications, 1961), 98; hereafter cited in text as *Journals*.

5. Edwin Way Teale, ed., *The Wilderness World of John Muir* (Boston: Houghton Mifflin, 1982), xiii; hereafter cited in text as *Wilderness*.

6. Stephen Fox, *John Muir and His Legacy* (Boston: Little, Brown, 1981), 44; hereafter cited in text.

7. Aldo Leopold, *A Sand County Almanac* (New York: Ballantine Books, 1966), 111; hereafter cited in text.

8. Henry Beston, *The Outermost House* (New York: Penguin Books, 1988), 168; hereafter cited in text.

9. Jonathan Schell, *The Fate of the Earth* (New York: Avon Books, 1982), 105; hereafter cited in text as Schell.

10. Scripps College Commencement Speech, June 1962; hereafter cited in text as Scripps. In Beinecke papers.

11. Bill McKibben, *The End of Nature* (New York: Doubleday, 1989), 18; hereafter cited in text.

12. Bill Devall and George Sessions, *Deep Ecology* (Salt Lake City: Peregrine Smith Books, 1985), 65; hereafter cited in text.

13. John McPhee, *The Control of Nature* (New York: Farrar, Straus and Giroux, 1989), 7; hereafter cited in text.

14. Ynestra King, *What is Ecofeminism?* (New York: Ecofeminist Resources, 1990), 13; hereafter cited in text.

15. Rachel L. Bagby, "Building the Green Movement," *Women of Power* 9 (Spring 1988), 14.

16. Carolyn Merchant, *The Death of Nature* (San Francisco: Harper and Row, 1989), 164.

Selected Bibliography

PRIMARY WORKS
Rachel Carson's early stories, college themes, letters, research materials and notes, and working drafts were left by Carson to Yale University, where they are housed in the Rachel Carson Collection at the Beinecke Rare Book and Manuscript Library.

Books

The Edge of the Sea. 1955. Reprint. Boston: Houghton Mifflin, 1983.

The Sea around Us. Rev. ed. 1961. Reprint. New York: Oxford University Press, 1989.

A Sense of Wonder. New York. Harper and Row, 1965. First published as "Help Your Child to Wonder." *Woman's Home Companion*, July 1956.

Silent Spring. Boston: Houghton Mifflin, 1962.

Under the Sea Wind. New York: Dutton, 1941.

Magazine Articles

"The Bat Knew It First." *Colliers*, 18 November 1944, 24.

"Rachel Carson Answers Her Critics." *Audubon Magazine*, September 1963, 262-65, 313-15.

"Undersea." *Atlantic Monthly*, September 1937, 322-25. Reprinted in Paul Brooks, *The House of Life: Rachel Carson at Work*, 22-29. Boston: Houghton Mifflin, 1989.

Pamphlets

Bear River: A National Wildlife Refuge. Conservation in Action, no. 8. Washington, D.C.: Government Printing Office, 1950.

Chincoteague: A National Wildlife Refuge. Conservation in Action, no. 1. Washington, D.C.: Government Printing Office, 1947.

Guarding Our Wildlife Resources. Conservation in Action, no. 5. Washington, D.C.: Government Printing Office, 1948.

Mattamuskeet: A National Wildlife Refuge. Conservation in Action, no. 4. Washington, D.C.: Government Printing Office, 1947.

Parker River: A National Wildlife Refuge. Conservation in Action, no. 2. Washington, D.C.: Government Printing Office, 1947.

SECONDARY WORKS

Books and Parts of Books

Anticaglia, Elizabeth. "Rachel Carson." In *Twelve American Women*, 208-24. Chicago: Nelson-Hall, 1975.

Bartram, William. *Travels*. New York: Penguin Books, 1988.

Beston, Henry. *The Outermost House*. New York: Penguin Books, 1988.

Brooks, Paul. *The House of Life: Rachel Carson at Work*. 1972. Reprint. Boston: Houghton Mifflin, 1989.

_____. *Speaking for Nature: How Literary Naturalists from Henry Thoreau to Rachel Carson Have Shaped America*. Boston: Houghton Mifflin, 1980.

Devall, Bill, and George Sessions. *Deep Ecology*. Salt Lake City: Peregrine Smith Books, 1985.

Diamond, Irene, and Gloria Feman Orenstein. *Reweaving the World*. San Francisco: Sierra Club Books, 1990.

Downs, Robert B. "Upsetting the Balance of Nature." In *Books That Changed America*, 260-288. New York: Macmillan, 1970.

Farnes, Patrica, and G. Kass-Simon, eds. *Women of Science: Righting the Record*. Bloomington: Indiana University Press, 1990.

Fordham, Frieda. *An Introduction to Jung's Psychology*. Baltimore: Penguin Books, 1966.

Fox, Stephen. *John Muir and His Legacy*. Boston: Little, Brown, 1981.

Gartner, Carol B. *Rachel Carson*. New York: Frederick Ungar Publishing, 1983.

Gilford, Henry. *Heroines of America*. New York: Fleet Press, 1970.

Graham, Frank, Jr. *Since Silent Spring*. Boston: Houghton Mifflin, 1970.

Hynes, H. Patricia. *The Recurring Silent Spring*. New York: Pergamon Press, 1989.

King, Ynestra. *What is Ecofeminism?* New York: Ecofeminist Resources, 1990.

Leopold, Aldo. *A Sand County Almanac*. New York: Ballantine Books, 1966.

McKibben, Bill. *The End of Nature*. New York: Doubleday, 1989.

McPhee, John. *The Control of Nature*. New York: Farrar, Straus and Giroux, 1989.

Merchant, Carolyn. *The Death of Nature*. San Francisco: Harper and Row, 1989.

Muir, John. *Wilderness Essays*. Salt Lake City: Peregrine Smith Books, 1988.

Rossiter, Margaret W. *Women Scientists in America*. Baltimore: Johns Hopkins University Press, 1982.

Schell, Jonathan. *The Fate of the Earth*. New York: Avon Books, 1982.

Shepard, Odell, ed. *The Heart of Thoreau's Journals.* New York: Dover Publications, 1961.

Sterling, Philip. *Sea and Earth: The Life of Rachel Carson.* New York: Thomas Y. Crowell, 1970.

Teale, Edwin Way. *The Wilderness World of John Muir.* Boston: Houghton Mifflin, 1982.

Thoreau, Henry David. *Walden.* New York: New American Library, 1960.

Whorton, James. *Before Silent Spring: Pesticides and Public Health in Pre-DDT America.* Princeton, N.J.: Princeton University Press, 1974.

Articles and Pamphlets

Briggs, Shirley A. *Silent Spring: A View from 1987.* Chevy Chase, Md.: Rachel Carson Council, 1987.

Brooks, Paul. "The Courage of Rachel Carson." *Audubon* 89 (January 1987): 12, 14-15.

Coates, Ruth Allison. "Rachel Carson." *Great American Naturalists.* Minneapolis: Lerner Publications, 1974.

Fulford, Robert. "When Jane Jacobs Took on the World." *New York Times Book Review,* 16 February 1992, 3, 28.

Hines, Bob. "Remembering Rachel." *Yankee Magazine* (June 1991): 62-66.

Hynes, H. Patricia. "Catalysts of the American Environmental Movement." *Women of Power* 9 (Spring 1988): 37-41, 78-80.

McCurdy, Patrick P. "Twenty-Five Years after Rachel Carson." *Chemical Week* 139 (20 August 1986): 3.

McKibben, Bill. "The Mountain Hedonist." *New York Review,* 11 April 1991, 29-32.

Norman, Geoffrey. "The Flight of Rachel Carson." *Recorder: The Chatham Alumnae Magazine* 54, 2 (Spring 1985): 4-8.

Norwood, Vera. "The Nature of Knowing: Rachel Carson and the American Environment." *Signs* 12 (Summer 1987): 740-60.

Seif, Dorothy Thompson. "How I Remember Rachel." *Recorder: The Chatham Alumnae Magazine* 54, no. 2 (Spring 1985): 9.

Taped Interview

"Rachel Carson Speaks about *Silent Spring.*" 14 December 1962. The Rachel Carson Council, Chevy Chase, Md.

Manuscript Collections

The Rachel Carson Collection, Beinecke Library, Yale University, New Haven, Conn.

The Rachel Carson Council, Chevy Chase, Md.

Index

The Author

Mary A. McCay, chair of the English department at Loyola University in New Orleans, holds an M.A. in English from Boston College and a Ph.D. in English, with an emphasis in American Studies, from Tufts University. She was a visiting professor at the Catholic University of Nijmegen in the Netherlands and a Fulbright professor at Keele University in the United Kingdom. She served as a contributing editor to the *Feminist Companion to Literature in English*, for which she wrote the entry on Rachel Carson, and wrote the introduction to the Easton Press edition of *Silent Spring*. She has lectured extensively on Rachel Carson and her work.

The Editor

Warren French (Ph. D., University of Texas, Austin) retired from Indiana University in 1986 and is now an honorary professor associated with the Board of American Studies at the University College of Swansea, Wales. In 1985 Ohio University awarded him a doctor of humane letters. He has contributed volumes to Twayne's United States Authors Series on Jack Kerouac, Frank Norris, John Steinbeck, and J. D. Salinger. His most recent publication for Twayne is *The San Francisco Poetry Renaissance, 1955-1960.*

Warren French, Editor
University College of Swansea, Wales